ADHD

Learning to Thrive Through the Mindfulness and
Act Approach Made Simple

(A Family Resource for Helping Yourself Succeed
With Adhd)

Jerrold Applewhite

Published by Rob Miles

© **Jerrold Applewhite**

All Rights Reserved

Adhd: Learning to Thrive Through the Mindfulness and Act Approach Made Simple (A Family Resource for Helping Yourself Succeed With Adhd)

ISBN 978-1-990084-15-7

ISBN 978-1-990084-15-7

Legal & Disclaimer

Table of Contents

INTRODUCTION 1

CHAPTER 1: IS ADHD A MENTAL DISORDER? A LEARNING DISORDER? SOMETHING ELSE ENTIRELY? 3

CHAPTER 2: THINGS TO CONSIDER BEFORE GOING DOWN THE ROUTE OF SPECIALIST SERVICES 7

CHAPTER 3: EARLY DETECTION 12

CHAPTER 4: GOOD NEWS: MYRIAD TREATMENTS 20

CHAPTER 5: SYMPTOMS OF ADHD 28

CHAPTER 6: ADHD PARENTING TIPS 33

CHAPTER 7: USING BEHAVIOR MANAGEMENT THERAPY 42

CHAPTER 8: CHANGES IN DIETS FOR CHILDREN WITH ADHD CAN HELP 48

CHAPTER 9: ADHD: DIAGNOSIS AND TREATMENT 53

CHAPTER 10: SKILL BUILDING ACTIVITIES 66

CHAPTER 11: CAUSES OF ADHD 74

CHAPTER 12: PARENTING ADHD CHILDREN 78

CHAPTER 13: THE BENEFITS OF ADHD 85

CHAPTER 14: ATTENTION DEFICIT DISORDER: IS IT REALLY THAT? 95

CHAPTER 15: ADULT SUFFERS OF ADHD 103

CHAPTER 16: WHAT IS ADD / ADHD? 110

CHAPTER 17: THE ROLE OF OMEGA-3 FATTY ACIDS 117

CHAPTER 18: WHERE DOES MY CHILD SHINE? 125

CHAPTER 19: ENCOURAGE YOUR CHILD TO MAKE FRIENDS, MOVE RIGHT, AND SLEEP ON TIME 135

CHAPTER 20: NATURAL AND ALTERNATIVE REMEDIES .. 139

CHAPTER 21: THE RELATIONSHIP BETWEEN CAFFEINE & ADHD 146

CHAPTER 22: BUILDING MINDSET 153

CHAPTER 24: CAN CHILDREN WITH ADHD GET BETTER? 172

CHAPTER 25: THE DANGERS OF USING CBD OIL IN AN INDIVIDUAL WITH ADHD 180

CONCLUSIONS 184

Introduction

Adult ADHD can be difficult to live with—more difficult than those who don't have it will ever know. There are a lot of myths and misconceptions about adult ADHD, increasing the stigma around the disorder and making it harder for people to seek diagnoses and treatment.

Fortunately, the tide is shifting on public perceptions of mental illnesses and the people who suffer from them. More and more information is becoming available as researchers continue their work and the public grows more educated about the importance of mental health. With time and a bit of luck, those who suffer from this chemical imbalance and others like it will find it easier to learn about their conditions and seek the help they need.

For those living with adult ADHD, life can seem a perpetual struggle. Missed appointments, lost possessions, unpaid bills, and a general struggle to stay on top of life's many demands, even the simple ones, can have many feeling down and hopeless. However, there are everyday ways to cope with the symptoms and help make your life more manageable. In this short yet information-packed guide, you'll find tips for time management, organization, productivity, and coping with stress and interpersonal connections all catered specifically to the unique needs of those with adult ADHD.

While this book offers tons of advice, it is important to remember that this in no way substitutes for the medical guidance of a trained professional. Adult ADHD is a real, but treatable, medical condition, and those who have it should always stay in communication with their doctors to get the medical treatment that they need.

With that, I bid you welcome. I have a lot to share with you, and I'm excited to get started.

Chapter 1: Is Adhd A Mental Disorder? A Learning Disorder? Something Else Entirely?

Technically, ADHD is considered a mental disorder. It is also considered a learning disability. The good news is this disorder does not carry the same social stigma that comes with many other mental disorders. There are so many people living with and being diagnosed with this disorder today, that it is very commonplace and raises no eyebrows when it is mentioned. From a social perspective, this is great news for those suffering with ADHD.

From a medical perspective, this might not be such a blessing. Since the disorder is believed to affect so many people, there are some problems that sufferers come up against:

1. Some teachers are quick to diagnose children in their own minds without any testing to prove their theory. They may push parents toward medication or assume the disorder is to blame for all bad

behavior displayed in their classroom. ADHD medication is seen as the quick fix for children who do not sit quiet and do as they are told perfectly. This can be dangerous. Please read more about ADHD and the school system in chapter four.

2. Parents sometimes struggle to find doctors willing to take their concerns about ADHD seriously. Some doctors will downplay the symptoms reported by parents, while others are too eager to prescribe mediation without properly evaluating and diagnosing the child. Parents have to jump through hoops to make sure their child is properly diagnosed, since there are other mental disorders that can exhibit many of the same symptoms. As you will discover in the final chapter of this book, sometimes ADHD will be present along with another mental or learning disorder.

3. Adults are not always taken seriously when they tell medical professionals they want to be tested for ADHD. It is believed that around 60% of ADHD children carry

the disorder into adulthood, and many never receive a proper diagnosis. Read chapter eleven to learn more about the disorder as it relates to the work life of adult sufferers. It is very similar to what children go through at school, but your boss is much less likely to recommend treatment than a teacher in elementary school.

4. There is a lot of confusion over the use of medication to treat ADHD. Some are against it, others are scared of it, and still others are too casual in its use. Read chapter seven to understand what medications are typically prescribed and what risks may come with them for adults and children.

On one hand, diagnosing ADHD is very easy and is done every day. On the other hand, it may be so common today that many medical professionals no longer realize how serious it is for the sufferer. It is on the adult sufferer or the parent of a sufferer to seek out professionals who can properly diagnose and treat the disorder.

Chapter 2: Things To Consider Before Going Down The Route Of Specialist Services

Conceivable reasons for ADHD type behaviors

Any issue that causes real uneasiness in the kid can bring about behavioral issues. Along these lines it is useful to ask a general expert do an essential screen for signs and manifestations of conditions, for example, anemia, glue ear, asthma, and constipation (including examinations a fundamental blood screen, peek flow, and otoscopy). Any issue that causes mental inconvenience can likewise bring about behavioral issues; in this manner it merits inquiring about life events, parental prosperity, school issues, (for example, harassing and/or learning troubles) and peer group issues.

If the above are discounted, it merits attempting some straightforward techniques that may have a constructive outcome to the kid and their family, and that can be considered, where suitable, before making a referral for master ADHD appraisal and treatment.

Basic things to attempt

1. Daily meal plan and nourishment: Currently, kids' eating regimens are high in sugars, fats, and salt and low in fiber, vitamins, minerals, and key unsaturated fats. There are three parts to enhancing kids' nourishment that have confirmation to bolster them enhancing their psychological well-being, learning and conduct.

Eliminate potential aggravations – have a go at expelling every single artificial additives and consider issues like lactose intolerance.

Add any missing supplements - attempt a day by day multi-vitamin and mineral supplement and EPA rich Omega-3 crucial unsaturated fats.

Balance the eating routine – decrease sugars and saturated fats, expand complex starches (which manage glucose levels) and fiber (through raw fruits and vegetables), and have three adjusted meal plan a day (breakfast is especially imperative).

2. Natural air and work out: Accentuate the significance of a lot of activity for kids, especially outside in green spaces, including chances for unstructured, unsupervised play.

3. The significance of solid, secure relationships: Parents need to work truly hard to develop positive associations with their kids, especially when there are behavioral issues. Relationships can get focused by elevated amounts of antagonism between a parent and kid, bringing about on-going negative fortification, which further harms the nature of the relationship. By endeavoring to notice, comment on, connect and acclaim their kid as regularly as possible, kids can build better self-regard. Encourage parents to have clear and quick results for undesirable conduct and endeavor to adhere to these and not give in, to stay firm and try to avoid panicking. Encourage them to abstain from getting drawn into controversy, which typically stokes the flame, exacerbating things.

4. Normal positive family time: To keep some positive family encounter going, parents ought to make occasions for their family to appreciate each others' conversation, for example, going out together as a family consistently and having no less than one dinner a day together.

5. Correspondence and comprehension: Urge relatives to converse with each other, yet all the more critically hear each other out. Urge parents to request and endeavor to comprehend their kid's perspective and help the kid comprehend the parents. Be cognizant to more extensive family or parental despondency or struggle. In the event that there are uncertain challenges between the parents, then these will frequently demonstrate themselves through the passionate state and conduct of their kids. Here, irregularity between guardians can turn into an impediment to advance. You can meet with both parents and not only the parent who brought the kid. Attempt to accumulate the legitimate perspectives of both parents (without their kid being available) and help them to remember the significance of both parents settling on choices together and imparting these to their kids.

Chapter 3: Early Detection

The National Institute of Mental Health (NIMH) and the American Psychiatric Association (APA) recognize three main sub-types of ADHD. People who suffer from predominantly inattentive ADHD tend to exhibit more distractedness, forgetfulness, and general inattentive behavior. They may not seem as hyperactive or as impulsive. For this reason, these people may go undiagnosed. After all, it would appear, upon first glance, that they lack half of the key symptoms associated with the condition. Children who suffer from this subtype are more likely to get labeled as "lazy."

People who suffer from predominately hyperactive-impulsive ADHD tend toward the opposite side of the spectrum. Their condition is marked by restlessness, high-energy, and frequently immature or even destructive behavior. Just as the predominately inattentive sub-type can easily go undiagnosed, so too can the predominately hyperactive-impulsive sub-type. Children who suffer from this sub-type are more likely to be labeled as "bad" kids or "behavior problems."

Finally, children (or adults) who exhibit a combination of both inattentive and hyperactive-impulsive traits fall into the combined sub-type. This is the most easily diagnosed of the sub-types, as it speaks to both sides of the condition. It is, therefore, easier for laymen and professionals alike to see that the exhibited symptoms can be chalked up to ADHD.

Understanding the various subtypes is key when considering early signs and early detection. After all, it's important to know that not every child who suffers from the condition is going to be a "classic" case. Sometimes, you have to look more closely at what their behaviors and experiences are before you can be sure whether or not they suffer from ADHD. After all, labeling a child as "lazy" or "bad" will only serve to stunt their emotional, social, and academic development. Seeing the condition for what it is and getting them help is the best way to secure for them a bright future.

First and foremost, let's be clear that when we talk about "early detection," there's such a thing as diagnosing a child too early. After all, signs and symptoms of ADHD in children range from trouble sharing, trouble taking turns, an inability to finish activities, fidgeting, emotional outbursts, forgetfulness, and not listening (which can sometimes be recognized by a failure to make eye contact). Stop me if this doesn't sound like about 80% of the toddlers in America. At a certain age, ADHD symptoms are not "symptoms" but natural stages in regular child development. The concern comes when the child does not grow past these behaviors.

Parents are often the first to notice when something is wrong. After all, you're caring for your child every day and it becomes easy to tell when a behavior is persistent or just a phase. I knew that something wasn't right even when Kade was very young. He struggles in school and he had consistent and violent tantrums. As much as it pains me to say it, there were days when I had difficulty being the patient and loving parent that I wanted to be. After watching his behavior carefully and doing my research on ADHD, I was able to finally understand that Kade's brain worked differently than the those of his peers. I was able to identify those triggers that were more likely to set him off and devise ways to avoid them. In short, the best early detection for ADHD is being an attentive and loving parent who takes the time to learn about the condition and how it presents itself.

Kade is now 10 years old and he and I are still learning about his condition. Every day may present new struggles and challenges, but also new joys. I'm grateful that I was able to see his condition for what it was early enough to be able to make some real and lasting positive changes in his life.

7. Planning The Day For Adults

Facts appear to become useless to individual grown ups that are suffering from ADHD (ADD). We all have our goals obvious within our minds, and can't wait to be accomplished, wishing that there is a way to skip everything needed to become completed in the procedure. Sadly enough, this attitude has a tendency to get us stressed, if we are to begin the work. We appear to be aware what we would like from the finish, without getting any concept of what must be done at the start.

This story holds true for that everyday existence too. Grown ups struggling with ADD, generally start a full day ensuring of the goals, however they can't appear to have their focal points right and choose how to start from. This will cause them to feel stressed and guilty, causing them to be feel below par, and eventually work less.

To prevent this type of situation, these grown ups should get the practice of creating a daily planning routine.

To be able to develop this type of routine, the next 3 steps could be practiced:

1. Determining On the Time for you to Perform the Planning

Time during the day once the planning process can be achieved ought to be made the decision first. This will require no more than fifteen minutes, and also the time could be either set particularly (say 8:00 PM) or might just be something similar to time "before bed."

Time late within the day is generally most liked by the grown ups with ADD, since that's when they're probably the most alert. This really is useful because it enables someone to plan for the following day, rather than worrying regarding this once they should retire for the night!

2. Looking at the To-Do List

First of all make certain that you simply do make use of a to-do list, (should you not make one). This is often examined throughout all of your planning periods, to help remind you of the items must be done. It may also help you feel better about the only thing you have previously done throughout your day.

You have to regularly re-write their email list, removing all of the completed tasks and adding them. Probably the most urgent and important from the tasks ought to be noted towards the top of their email list. You might break the big ones into 3-5 steps, observing it lower in your list.

3. Looking at the Calendar

Now, undergo your everyday planner (presuming that you're now finally one!). Look at your next day's visits and include individuals occasions around the planner, not failing to remember the travel time. You can now plan how you can put aside a number of your remaining time for the jobs across the to-do list.

Thus, investing just fifteen minutes on planning the schedule can get rid of the everyday stress in the existence of the adult with ADD, and may help one proceed.

Chapter 4: Good News: Myriad Treatments

So, you or a loved one has been diagnosed with ADHD. Now what? The good news is that there are many treatment options out there for kids and adults. Medication, therapy or behavioral interventions whether alone or in combination can dramatically improve the lives of the person living with ADHD and the people who love them.

Medication

In the early years of ADHD treatment, there were few choices for management with medications. Today there are a number of medications available that can make a significant difference in the lives of people with ADHD. While a discussion of each medication is beyond the scope of this book, a brief description of each category is offered.

Stimulant medications are probably the best known of the medications used to treat ADHD. This type of medication has been used for several decades. Stimulant medications can help with focusing attention and ignoring distractions. They work in about 70% - 80% of people. Some of the most commonly used medications in this category include Adderall, Focalin, Ritalin, Vyvanse and Concerta. ("Drugs Used", 2015)

Non-stimulant medications can improve concentration and impulse control. They are often used when stimulant medications doesn't work or cannot be used due to side effects. Some of the commonly used non-stimulants include Strattera, Kapvay and Intuniv. Other types of medications including some anti-depressants and anti-hypertensives may be used in the treatment of ADHD. ("Drugs Used", 2015)

The decision to use medication is not to be taken lightly. Medication is not a quick fix. The decision of when or if to use medication is best made with your doctor. Not all doctors will prescribe medication for ADHD. You primary healthcare provider may refer you to a psychiatrist who specializes in ADHD. Ask lots of questions and don't be afraid to voice your concerns. Making the decision with your healthcare provider will help you to determine the right path for you or your loved one.

Behavioral Interventions

For some people, medication is not the best solution for any number of reasons. Certain types of therapy have been shown to be effective in the management of ADHD.

Behavioral Therapy (sometimes referred to as behavior management) has also proven to be most effective in the management of ADHD for both children and adults. Behavioral treatments have been successfully used in the management of disruptive behavior, inattention, social skills building and work or academic performance (Block & Smith, 2016). Other types of therapy have not proven effective for ADHD.

The goal of behavioral therapy is to establish new, productive and positive behaviors while eliminating (sometimes called "extinguishing") unwanted behaviors through the use of contingencies and reinforcement. That's a fancy way of saying that positive behaviors are rewarded, negative behaviors have consequences. Behavior therapy addresses specific behaviors by setting specific goals or expectations, establishing routines, using rewards and consequences and increasing positive attention. Behavioral therapy may include the person with ADHD, parents, spouses, teachers or other significant people in the person's life.

Environmental/Lifestyle Interventions

A person's lifestyle can play a tremendous role in managing ADHD. Research has found that making good lifestyle choices has a huge effect on ADHD symptoms. So what does that mean exactly? Simple things like eating well, getting enough sleep, being active and managing stress can make getting through the day much smoother.

Exercising is one of the most effective ways to manage symptoms. Physical activity triggers an increase in the brain's dopamine, norepinephrine, and serotonin levels which in turn affect focus and attention (Block & Smith, 2016). They are also some of the same brain chemicals that help manage our mood.

Sleeping can have a huge effect on ADHD symptoms. Not just any sleep but that good deep sleep that lets us awake refreshed and ready for the day. Interestingly, adults and children respond to lack of sleep differently. Adults tend to become tired, sluggish and inattentive. Children tend to become more active, distracted and oppositional ("ADHD & Sleep," n.d.) For a person already dealing with inattention or hyperactivity, a lack of sleep can make it much harder to manage symptoms.

Eating a well-balanced diet also helps with symptom management. Key nutrients such as zinc, iron and magnesium have been found to play a role in ADHD (Villagomes & Ramtekkar, 2014). Omega-3 fatty acids have been found to improve symptoms of hyperactivity, impulsivity, and concentration in kids and adults (Sinn, Milte & Howe, 2010).

The Best Treatment

So what treatment works best? The short answer is the one that is right for you or your loved one. The more complete answer is something called multi-modal treatment. Multi-modal treatment is the combining of treatment interventions to achieve optimum outcome which in this case is symptom reduction.

For ADHD, three types of treatment have been shown to be most effective: medication, behavioral therapy and a combination of medication and behavioral interventions including educational supports and lifestyle management. In fact, a National Institute of Mental Health (NIMH) study that included over 600 children with ADHD found that medication accounted for the largest improvement in ADHD symptoms. The addition of behavior treatments resulted in even more improvement and normalization of behavior. (MTA Study, 1999).

If you think that you or someone you love may be struggling with attention issues, the first step is to see a healthcare professional who can make an accurate diagnosis. A good place to start is your primary care physician. He or she may be able to make the diagnosis or may make an appropriate referral to a psychiatrist, psychologist and/or therapist. Once the diagnosis is made, the discussion can turn to treatment options.

Along with clinical treatment options, there are a number of strategies that can help people with ADHD, and the ones who love them, cope with the challenges that come with having attention issues. The next part of the book offers specific strategies for dealing with ADHD whether you are the person with ADHD, a parent of a child with ADHD or you are in a relationship with someone who has ADHD.

Chapter 5: Symptoms Of Adhd

ADHD is typically characterized by a lack of focus, impulsive behavior and hyperactivity. These symptoms vary from one individual to another and depend on the circumstances.

For instance, some people with ADHD cannot focus on anything whereas some other people can be extremely focused on something they find interesting.

Also, some individuals may have difficulty with being in a relationship and thus appear to be antisocial whereas some others may show a completely opposite behavior, going from one relationship into another. Some other problems and behavior patterns that stem from ADHD include the following:

anxiety

mood swings

depression

chronic boredom

poor organizational skills

impulsiveness

difficulty controlling anger

low self-esteem

low frustration tolerance

This lack of focus is the main problem leading to many other difficulties. People suffering from ADHD may have hard time concentrating on their job or everyday tasks, they get easily distracted, they may forget appointments, deadlines, important dates, and thus risk offending someone.

Moreover, they may have troubles dealing with time, such as not finishing projects on time, wasting time, or having a wrong perception of the passage of time. Also, people suffering from ADHD are usually bad drivers simply because there are so many things that should be paid attention to in the traffic.

However, it is not at all true that people with ADHD cannot focus, and thus it is probably better to say that in some cases these people have problems with shifting their attention. Sometimes, they can focus on certain things and when their focus center is turned on, they have difficulty recognizing anything else as important.

They can focus on things of personal interest or things that are novel to them, or appear to be challenging. However, this interest is only temporary, because once they master these challenges or become familiar with them, they lose interest because they are neither challenging nor novel any longer.

This impulsive behavior observed in adults may lead to making risky or impulsive decisions. Also, these people may have difficulties with getting on with other people, or being easily irritated, which may lead them to living a lonely life, consequently paving the way for depression.

This may all lead to having problems at work, problems in a relationship or marriage, feeling socially inappropriate, or being depressed. Consequently, this may lead to developing alcohol or drug addiction.

Even though these are the symptoms that most of us can relate to, they are taken to be the symptoms indicating ADHD when they become so severe and occur so often that they exhibit a negative influence on a person's life and everyday activities. With all these possible difficulties caused by ADHD in mind, it becomes pretty obvious that ADHD is a serious condition that should not be disregarded at all.

Since it is sometimes difficult to tell ADHD apart from a person's normal behavior patterns, it is important to seek professional help. Only a specialist can clearly tell you whether your symptoms are indicative of ADHD, other condition, or a combination of conditions.

When diagnosed with ADHD, you need to learn what your weaknesses and strengths are, so that you can create some strategies that will help you cope with your ADHD symptoms. The following chapters will give you a short account of the most common

ADHD symptoms and the proven ways that can help you manage these same symptoms and avoid their negative impact on other areas of your life.

Summary

ADHD is typically related to impulsive behavior, lack of focus and hyperactivity, which consequently may lead to a number of other difficulties and problems, preventing you from living a normal life.

Chapter 6: Adhd Parenting Tips

ADHD and the family

It can be very overwhelming for the parents to find out that their kid is suffering from ADHD. At the very onset, the parents feel scared and confused for they don't know what to do with such a kid. But, with a clear knowledge of ADHD and a little understanding, you can help your kid go through this.

The entire family is directly affected by the ADHD child. The family members might feel helpless when trying to deal with the child. In this case, a positive attitude, patience and the right techniques can go a long way in helping the entire family and also the child.

You, as a parent, need to understand that ADHD is as frustrating for the poor child as for you or your family members. You need to focus all your energies to help him. By helping him, you will help the entire family.

If you are looking for parenting tips to handle a child with ADHD, then the following tips and techniques will come handy:

Increasing movement

Children with ADHD have a lot of energy. You should constantly be on the lookout to help them utilize this energy. They need to be active so that they can use this energy in a good way. It is important that you encourage them to take part in physical activities that involve movement such as exercise and sports.

Physical activities will help the child with ADHD to be less anxious. It will help him to be more focussed.

Movement throughout the day will help him to channel his energies and this attention in the most positive of ways.

These activities will help them to stay away from depression and sadness.

Sticking to a routine

Children suffering from ADHD are not very fond of surprises. The kids can perform better when things happen in a routine and predictable manner. They are more likely to feel comfortable when things happen in a certain pattern.

The kid with ADHD should know what lies ahead of him, so it is important that a structure is devised and followed at home. A parent should make sure that there is routine in the way in which things happen around and with the kid. This will help the kid to stay organized and focussed. For example:

Set a time table for the kid. Make him understand the time table, so that he knows beforehand what to expect next.

The child should follow a pattern. For example, every night before going off to sleep, he should keep his morning clothes ready.

The child should have a definite time for food, play and homework.

Don't plan surprises for the kid. Make him do the same things at the same place. For example, set a time for his play and make him play at the same spot in the house.

When you set the time table, make sure that you give the kid enough time for everything. He should not struggle with time.

You have to consider the individual characteristics of the kid. You need to see if the schedule that you've set works for him or not. Make necessary changes if you feel that the child is struggling with the routine work. The idea is to make the kid happy and comfortable while sticking to his routine.

Place many clocks in the house and also make it a habit to set alarms for various activities.

You need to lead by example. You should be organized yourself to help your child.

Keep the house neat and organized. The kid should know what is kept where in the house.

You should inculcate the habit of cleanliness and organization in your child.

He should know that he needs to place everything at the right place.

Allocate a space for the child that is exclusively for him. This place should be different from where the child plays or does other activities. This exclusive place will serve like his refuge when he needs one.

Helping the child to eat right

Though food and the child's diet are not counted as one of the causes of ADHD in the child, but food can directly help the mental health of the kid. Food will help him to grow physically and mentally. This will have an effect on how he behaves and conducts himself.

It is known that if you closely monitor the diet of the child and make sure that he gets the right nutrients at the right time, you will be able to decrease the symptoms of ADHD in the child.

A child with ADHD can get very impulsive, which in turn will affect his food habits. You might notice that the child misses the meals or overeats at times. It is important that the parents at home and the teachers at the school make sure that the child is eating regularly and healthy meals.

The food should consist of fresh and healthy vegetables and fruits, instead of junk food. As a parent or teacher, you will have to understand that you can't trust the child with his food habits. He might not eat for many hours or might overeat whatever he finds interesting if you are not taking interest. You will have to take extra effort to understand the kid's erratic eating habits, so that you can personally monitor him. This will help the child on a physical, mental and emotional level.

You can make use of the following quick points while planning for meals for your child:

Make a proper schedule for the child's diet plan. Write it down on a chart paper and put it in the kitchen. Make the child understand that he should follow the schedule, even when he is in school.

Make sure that the schedule takes care of the nutritional requirements of the child. He should get enough proteins, carbohydrates, vitamins and minerals along with other nutrients.

You can even consult a nutritionist to come up with the diet plan.

Ensure that the child gets healthy food at regular intervals. He should not get a chance to overeat.

Make sure that the kid does not get fascinated by all the junk food advertisements. He should stay away from junk food.

If you're eating outside, you to take extra effort to make sure that the kid is not gorging on sugar laden unhealthy food.

Lead by example. Eat healthy food yourself and keep no junk food at home.

Helping the child to sleep better

A good sleep and sufficient rest is essential for everybody, but it is all the more important for a kid with ADHD. These kids need to sleep as much as any other kid, but their condition leads to overstimulation and makes it difficult for them to fall asleep.

You will have to ensure that your kid goes to bed early and gets sufficient rest. This will be challenging for you, but if you take the right precautions, you will be able to help your child sleep well. Here are some tips:

Help your kid to create an atmosphere where he can rest and sleep well.

You should decrease the time the kid spends watching television and increase the time he spends exercising. This will automatically help him to sleep better.

Make necessary changes in the diet of the kid with ADHD. Make sure that he is not having caffeine in excess quantities as that would disturb his sleep.

You can even try certain essential oils that have calming effect, such as the lavender oil. The aroma of the oils in the kid's room will help him to calm down.

You should also try the magic of love on your kids. It is said that if you spend around ten minutes hugging and cuddling the kid, it will help to calm him down.

Make sure that the kid is relaxed and calm at least one hour before going to bed. You should encourage him to spend the time before bed time in creative activities, such as drawing and colouring. Don't let him do anything that agitates his brain.

Calming music can also help the kid to sleep better. Kids with ADHD can get disturbed with too much noise, so you need to make sure that you put some calming music in the background. It is said that kids with ADHD find white noise calming. You can create an atmosphere of white noise, such as sound of the fan.

Chapter 7: Using Behavior Management Therapy

Behavior management therapy offers parents a variety of techniques that they can use to aid in parenting a child with ADHD. All of the techniques used in behavior management therapy are designed to help manage your child's symptoms, but they are not going to cure those symptoms. Behavior management therapy can be used with or without medication; the decision to medicate is entirely up to you and your child's doctor.

The goal of behavior management therapy is to change your behaviors as a parent so that you can successfully manage your child's behavior. Using the different techniques associated with behavior management therapy can help curb the destructive and embarrassing behaviors of your ADHD child, but will also improve your child's confidence levels as it shows them that they too can be successful.

What is behavior management therapy?
As we mentioned above behavior management therapy is a way for you to change your parenting behaviors and help control your ADHD child's impulsive behavior. With behavior management therapy there are two main principles, positive and negative reinforcement. Positive reinforcement involves rewarding and praising the good behavior, while negative reinforcement involves discouraging the bad behavior with appropriate consequences.

Behavior management therapy is a great way to teach your child that all of their actions have some kind of consequence, whether good or bad. With behavior management therapy you need to set specific rules and boundaries that your child is expected to follow. You also need to make sure that the outcome for following or not following the rules and boundaries are also clear, which means you as a parent must follow through with the consequences, no idle threats. In order for behavior management therapy to be effective it must be used in every aspect of your ADHD child's life.

Putting behavior management therapy to use

The first step to using behavior management therapy is to figure out what behaviors you can accept as a parent, and what behaviors are unacceptable. What you are trying to do here is to teach your child to think about their actions, as well as to control the impulse to act.

Using behavior management therapy is not going to be easy, nor will you see results overnight. As a parent you are going to have to be patient, but you are also going to need to be strong and not give up. Once you decide what behaviors are acceptable and which ones are not, you have to stick to it. You cannot change your mind on a daily basis. Punishing a behavior one day and then allowing the same behavior the next day is going to confuse your child and create even more behavioral problems.

Creating   the   rules

Establishing clear and concise rules is vital when parenting a child with ADHD, as it allows your child to know what is expected from them. Getting your child to understand and follow the rules can be a bit tricky, but not impossible. Rewarding your child for following the rules and punishing them for not following them is the best way to make your intentions clear. For children with ADHD, repetition is key to learning how or how not to behave.

Rules should be simple and easy to follow, but you also need to allow your child to learn from the mistakes that they have made. Many ADHD children do not do well with change; any disruption in their schedule can cause problems. Often times children deal with these changes by exhibiting odd behaviors, ones that most of us don't find to be appropriate. You as a parent need to be flexible with these kinds of behaviors, if the behavior isn't destructive there is nothing wrong with allowing it to continue, many times the behavior is soothing to your child and allows them to deal with the changes.

No matter what rules you set and how well you follow the rules your child is going to have some kind of outburst. Outbursts are quite common in children with ADHD and are one of the biggest challenges that parents face. Outbursts often come at the least appropriate times and parents are left at a loss of what to do. What is important is that you take control immediately during an outburst. Bear in mind that taking control does not mean yelling and screaming at your child, that kind of behavior from the parent is only going to make things worse.

The best way to deal with an outburst is to institute a "time-out." Using "time-outs" is a great way to calm your child, as well as yourself down, but they must be used properly. Always explain to your child that "time-outs" are a way to allow your child to calm down, but while calming down they must also think about what they did wrong. When you use "time-outs" will depend on what kind of behaviors you have decided to allow compared to what you do not allow. Just keep in mind that some disruptive behavior should be expected, as that is just how kids with ADHD release their extra energy, but being overly disruptive on purpose should never be tolerated. If you are in public when one of these outbursts happen, quietly and calmly remove your child to a safe location.

Chapter 8: Changes In Diets For Children With Adhd Can Help

On the off chance that you need to help your child diminish some of those ADHD symptoms, you should try different things with what you're bolstering them. Since studies have demonstrated a connection amongst ADHD and what children eat, basically disposing of or including certain sustenance's may diminish symptoms or even dispose of them.

To me, changes in eating regimens for children with ADHD, is a great deal more desirable over professionally prescribed medications. That is on account of normal cures, for example, eat less carbs control, will get to the foundation of the issue instead of simply putting a band aid on it, which is precisely what the medications will do.

Keep in mind, a change to a sound eating routine is something worth being thankful for. There is no drawback to ADHD suggested diets that advance adhering to a good diet.

Here is an eating routine that my child's therapist recommended.

You have to take out these sustenances for two or three weeks:

Dairy Products-The most critical one to dispose of, from eating methodologies for children with adhd, is drain from a bovine. There are different creatures that deliver drain, yet I supplanted it with water. What's more, not only a glass or two. I had my child drink no less than 6 glasses for every day. Try not to cheat and give then kool-help or ice tea since they don't consider water. ADHD suggested diets, and so far as that is concerned all eating methodologies, incorporate bunches of water.

Yellow sustenances This will incorporate, yet not restricted to, corn, yellow beans, and yellow squash.

All garbage nourishment Say bye to potato chips, McDonalds, and everything else with no dietary esteem.

Fruit juices too much sugar. One glass of squeezed orange equivalents around six oranges.

Sugar-This is presumably the hardest one to kill since it's in such a large number of nourishments and beverages. On the off chance that you can't dispense with it 100%, come as close as possible. (Keep in mind it's just for two weeks)

Candy-particularly chocolate

Artificial sweeteners-incorporates saccharin, NutraSweet, aspartame I know, I know! That was your answer for no sugar right?

MSG-If you see this in the fixings, set back on the rack.

Processed meats-When you read the fixing mark and you can't articulate them, set it back on the rack.

Fried chicken-and whatever else that is seared.

Artificial sustenance colors They will be recorded as presumably Red, yellow, or blue color number whatever. Try not to touch them for the time being.

Once the two weeks are up you can begin returning these sustenance to your child's eating regimen in the following way.

Include one sustenance each other day. Eat however much of that sustenance as could reasonably be expected each day for four days. In the event that your child has an issue with one of the nourishments, you will see some sort of a "response" inside four days, for example, hives on the body, or ears turning splendid red, or even an expansion in hyperactivity. In the event that there's an issue, you'll know. On the off chance that there's no issue, you can incorporate that nourishment in ADHD suggested diets for your child.

Diets for children with ADHD ought to incorporate as much natural sustenance as you can bear the cost of in light of the fact that I know natural nourishment can be costly. Natural nourishment is developed without all the perilous enduring pesticides, herbicides and fungicides. Likewise incorporate a solid part of products of the soil your child's eating routine.

Dietary control is only one a player in an option treatment for ADHD. At the point when joined with home grown and homeopathy cures and behavioral treatment, common treatment can be similarly as viable and substantially more secure than physician recommended meds. I'm certain your child or girl will thank you later on for the common approach.

Chapter 9: Adhd: Diagnosis And Treatment

Looked at in isolation, ADHD symptoms are hardly abnormal. Most people experience symptoms such as feeling unfocused, scattered, and distracted. This does not mean because you are unfocused and scattered, you need ADHD treatment. It is very easy to confuse ADHD with other problems like emotional issues or learning disabilities that need different treatments.

To diagnose ADHD, it is important to get proper testing that will actually point out that what you have is really ADHD before you even start thinking about ADHD treatment. Unfortunately, there is no single physical, medical, or other type of test to succinctly diagnose ADHD. To determine if you or your child is ADHD, you will have to seek professional help.

Doctors and health professionals use a couple of different tools to determine if you are ADHD. This includes:

Asking you questions about your present and past problems

Checking your symptoms

Carrying out a medical exam to rule out other illnesses that can cause the same symptoms

Making the ADHD Diagnosis

ADHD appears to be different in every person. This means health professionals use a wide range of criteria to reach a diagnosis. To get an accurate evaluation, you must be very honest with your physician.

To receive an ADHD diagnosis, you must display some strong ADHD trademark symptoms like impulsivity, hyperactivity, or inattention. The mental health professional assess the problem by asking the following questions:

When did your symptoms start? The physician will want to know ADHD started manifesting because ADHD starts at childhood. If you cannot trace it back to your childhood, you may not be suffering from ADHD.

How severe are your symptoms? To receive an ADHD diagnosed, your symptoms must negatively affect your life. For example, ADHD symptoms can cause major problems in your finances, career, or even family responsibilities.

How long have you had the symptoms? To receive an ADHD diagnosis, symptoms must have been there for more than 6 months.

When and where do your symptoms appear? Your ADHD symptoms must appear in multiple settings like at school and at home. If it appears in only one environment setting, then it might not be ADHD.

Should You Be Evaluated for Adult ADHD

It is advisable to undergo adult ADHD evaluation if you have significant problems in the following areas:

Work or school: If you are not performing to the best of your ability

Relationship: If you start forgetting important things like anniversaries, experience inability to finish different tasks, or getting upset over little things

Career or job: quitting and frequently losing jobs

Emotions: when you have constant stress and worry because of responsibilities and the failure to meet goals

Day to day task: When you are unable to be responsible and pay your bills on time, inability to do household chores, and organize yourself.

After proper evaluation, you can finally get a clear diagnosis and then move to treatment if the diagnosis points to ADHD.

ADHD Treatments and Help

ADHD cannot be cured; however, but it can be fruitfully managed. Work with your physician to come up with individualized long-term plans for your child.

What is the ADHD treatment goal? The main goal for this treatment is to enable your child to learn how to control behavior on themselves and at the same time, teach your family how to create an atmosphere conducive for the treatment to work.

The best ADHD treatment for children requires close follow up and monitoring from health professionals and parents. A combination of behavior therapy and medicine is one of the best ways to treat ADHD.

Let us now look at each of them:

Medication

For most ADHD children, ADHD medication reduces impulsivity and hyperactivity. It also improves a child's ability to work, learn, focus, and improves physical coordination. Let us now look at the different types of medication used to treat ADHD in children:

Stimulants

This type of treatment has been in use for more than 50 years in the fight against ADHD. Stimulants are popular for having a calming effect on affected children.

Stimulants mostly come in diverse forms such asliquid, capsule, pill, and skin patch.

Stimulant medication falls into various categories such as short-acting, long acting, or the extended variety. All these categories have the same active ingredient; the only difference is the timing of their release into your body.

Long acting: means the medication will last longer in the body because it is slowly released in the body.

Extended release: means a limited amount of the medication is regularly released into the body over a certain period.

Short acting: means the medication stays in your child's body for a shorter period.

List of Stimulant Medications and their Approved Ages

Below is a List of Stimulant Medications with their approved age use:

Dexedrine or dextroamphetamine can be used for children aged 3 years and above

Adderall or amphetamine can be used on children aged three years and above

Concerta or methylphenidate can be used on children aged 6 years and above

Desoxyn or methamphetamine hydrochloride used on children aged 6 years and above

Possible Side Effects

Almost all medications have side effects; stimulants are not an exception to this rule. Here, we are going to highlight the list of possible side effects you can expect when your child uses this medication

Sleeping problems

Stomach aches

Insomnia

Decreased appetite

Irritability

Anxiety

Mild headaches

Non-Stimulants

Non-stimulants are the other types of medicine used to treat ADHD. Non-stimulant medications are a good alternative to stimulants because they have fewer side effects and can last up to 24 hours. You can combine them with a stimulant as a means to effective ADHD treatment.

Antidepressants

Antidepressants can sometime be effective at treating ADHD. However, they not as popular as non-stimulants and stimulants because the usage of antidepressants increases the risk of suicide among children and teens. If your doctor recommends antidepressant as a treatment for ADHD in your child, make sure to discuss the risks with the doctor.

ADHD children respond differently to different medication. One type of medicine may be perfect for child A but terrible for child B. With the aforementioned variety, you and your doctor can work together to find what medication or medication combination best suits your child.

Behavioral Therapy

Behavioral therapy, also known as behavior modification, is a very successful ADHD treatment for children. This type of treatment works better when you combine it with stimulant medications. Some ADHD individuals admit to reducing their medication after trying behavioral therapy.

This therapy tries to change your child's behavioral patterns by:

Giving your child clear directions and commands

Reorganizing your child's home and school environment

Laying down systems that reward a child's appropriate behavior and punish inappropriate behavior. For example, a teacher may reward an ADHD child for raising his/her hand in class instead of shouting out an answer or a comment.

This encourages the child to adopt the behavior.

Behavioral Therapy Strategies for You and Your Child

Check out the following behavioral strategies that will help your ADHD child

Create a routine: You should ensure your child follows the same routine every day by laying down a schedule for each day and placing it at a place where your child can read it and see what you and others expect of him/her throughout the day.

Avoiding distractions: Make sure nothing distracts your child from accomplishing his/her daily routines. A good example is turning off the radio and TV when your child is doing homework.

Lay down goals, and accordingly reward for your child's accomplishments: Write down realistic baby steps goals for your child and then reward him or her when he or she achieves them.

Effectively discipline inappropriate behavior: Stop yelling at, or spanking your child when he or she is in the wrong; instead, use better disciplinary measures such as using time outs and denying them privileges like playing with their best toys.

Give your child a choice: To help your child avoid over-stimulation from numerous activities, give the child ultimatums aimed at helping the child focus on one thing. Tell them to choose between watching television and playing with toys.

Get the child organized: Start by putting their things the same place every day until your child understands what belongs where. This will easily reduce the child's rate of losing things like toys, school bags, and clothing.

Alternative Treatments

Medication and behavioral therapy are the only scientifically proven ADHD therapies. However, as we previously saw, every child responds to ADHD treatments differently; thus, your doctor may recommend other additional treatments methods. These alternative therapies and treatments have not undergone careful medical studies and it is not certain if they clearly work. These treatments and therapy include:

Special education intervention such as occupational therapy or tutoring: This type of treatment helps your child improve physical coordination, energy control, hyperactivity, organization, and improves a child's ability to do everyday tasks.

The use of megavitamins therapy: This therapy denotes the use of massive amounts of vitamin C, vitamin B3, and vitamin B6 to treat schizophrenia because schizophrenia causes genetic abnormality and other forms of mental illnesses. By treating schizophrenia, you reduce the effects of ADHD.

Attention training: This involves hiring a professional to train your child how to focus on one thing at a time. This therapy helps your child deal with the symptoms of being unfocused.

Chiropractic treatment: Chiropractic treatment is a form of alternative medicine that mainly focuses on treating mechanical disorders of the spine and musculoskeletal systems with the aim of improving nervous system health. Chiropractic treatment restores optimal function in the nerve system. As you know, ADHD is a central nervous system disorder; therefore, this treatment can be an effective antidote.

The traditional talking psychotherapy: This method helps your child deal with his or her emotions. Here, a therapist or trusted individual encourages your child to talk about upsetting feelings; after talking about them, the therapist then teaches the child how to handle these feelings. This therapy builds your child's strength and helps your child feel good and positive about him or herself.

The above alternatives have no medical backing to prove their ability to cure ADHD. As such, before using any of them, consult your doctor.

Chapter 10: Skill Building Activities

All children have skills they need to learn through their childhood that help them become happy, healthy, productive adults. These skills are learned through modeling, peer interactions, trial and error, and specific training by adults in their lives. Most parents do not call these activities skill-building, but they are. A parent helps a teenager talk through a problem; that is skill-building. A parent helps a child make a choice and think about the consequences of that choice; that is skill-building. For kids with ADHD, interventions such as teachable moments, role modeling, and trial and error all have less impact on the child's learning given the struggle to stay focused long enough to learn the lesson. They also struggle with cause and effect. The result is the very skills they need the most to help them learn to manage and regulate their emotions and behaviors are the ones they have the least.

Research has shown that parenting with skill-building in mind can assist children with ADHD in learning these skills. The skills a child needs to learn vary somewhat from child to child but the keys one are

delayed gratification/impulse control

anger management

problem-solving skills

decision-making skills

social skills

Teaching these skills can be done the "typical" way that parents would teach any child with just some added emphasis and/or through the use of workbooks and worksheets. Parents can also seek professional help if they believe they need assistance in teaching these skills. Finally, school counselors often work with children to learn these skills in the school setting and can be a good resource.

Delayed Gratification teaches children to give up an instant desire in favor of achieving a more long-term goal. A research study left children in a room with a sweet on the plate. When the adult returned, they got two if they did not eat the candy. If they did eat, they were not in trouble, but they did not get a second one. This is an example of being able to use delayed gratification. Research shows that children who can cope with frustration and use delayed gratification show better coping as adults.

Parents can help children work towards this through stop and think assisting them in thinking through their choices and the potential outcomes. Parents can use teachable moments, but they need to keep them short and concise like directions, or the child will lose focus and not learn. Parents can also play games with their children, where they have to wait and take turns.

Anger Management is one of the more difficult skills for any child to learn. For children with ADHD who often are frustrated with their inability to control their behaviors, this can be especially true. The children often come to label their feelings as "bad," which then frustrates them even more. The children may try and avoid their anger resulting in larger explosions when they do express it.

Several workbooks are available for children with anger issues, whether they have ADHD or not. The pencil and paper method works well for some children with ADHD. The key is for parents to express to their children what they do want them to do when angry. Role-playing and then acting out often help the child practice and learn. For very young children, a simple chant, "Hands in my pockets (as they put them there) and my feet on the ground (as the step with each foot)" can help them remember not to hit or kick when angry. Practicing walking away, going to their room, making "mad" faces can all be fun ways the parent can work with the child. The key is to focus on the behavior, not the child, and not the emotion. The child needs to learn that anger is a normal and manageable part of life.

Problem Solving is learning how to solve problems. Children with ADHD often have trouble with thinking things through and determining the best way to solve their problems. They impulsively grab the first idea they think of and act. Learning problem-solving means to learn how to do a step by step process that can include brainstorming, evaluating the potential solutions, and responding. The process can vary in number of steps and complexity based on the age of the child. Having simple outlines can help the child stay focused and complete the process. Parents can also "talk through" the process.

Problem-solving can also be used even after a child has attempted to solve a problem. The parent can assist the child through the steps and talking about how the outcome would have been different had they used these skills. Remember, this is not a school-based lesson. Do not correct the children's spelling or grammar if written problem solving is done. This will make the child less confident in their abilities and hurt rather than help them develop these skills. See resources list for potential outlines.

Decision Making much like problem-solving involves helping the child to think through a decision before impulsively acting. Again, various strategies can be used. However, the more important key is choosing a plan that works and is consistent. As the child matures and gains ability, other strategies can be presented, and the child and parent can discuss the different options and how they can be used. With ADHD, two common decision-making strategies are pros and cons and choices and consequences.

With pros and cons, the child thinks of the pros and cons of their decision. What are the good things if you eat the cookies? What could go wrong if you eat the cookies? For parents who have used Stop-Think-Ask, this is an expansion on what they are already doing. They are just being expected to give the questions more consideration.

Choices and consequences are a way for the child to connect actions to results. They can list the possible solutions/options for the decision. They can get as creative as they want. The idea, at this point, is more brainstorming than actual choices. Then they list the potential consequences for eating choice, good and bad. Looking at the consequences, they then choose the best decision.

Social Skills cover a wide array of interpersonal interaction skills that help children communicate, play, and interact with others. Learning social skills can help children with ADHD reduce anxiety and increase their confidence so that they can interact better with siblings and peers. Again teaching them should be based on instruction, modeling, and role-playing. Children with ADHD learn best by doing.

Social skills are often taught best in a group setting where the peers can give feedback controlled by an adult. Getting a child involved in group activities they have an interest in can help. Girl Scouts and Boy Scouts would be two examples, but the list is endless. A child with interest in bugs may join a bug or science club. Local libraries often have great group activities that combine learning and fun. These types of groups are usually structured and managed in a way that helps the child interact appropriately. Often leaders will allow parents to sit in if needed because of concerns about the child's potential behaviors.

Parents can also give their child tasks that will improve their social skills. The child can be asked to come up with a list of 5 to 10 strengths of a specific family member and then review with the parent. This teaches the child how to observe and focus on others. The child can also be asked to make a list of 5 to 10 of his/her strengths or interest. The parent then discusses how these can be used to help build and develop friendships. Finally, parents can help their child develop empathy by assisting them in realizing or doing acts of kindness or being sensitive to others.

Make sure to keep these teachable moments brief, to the point, and age-appropriate. As with everything with a child with ADHD, you need to stop before you lose their focus.

Chapter 11: Causes Of Adhd

Genetics and neurobiology seems to be the main causes of ADHD in children. Parents may ask: What went wrong? Have I done something to cause this? There is minimal compelling evidence today which says that ADHD can arise by purely social factors or methods of raising children. Most legitimate reasons appear to fall under the realm of neurobiology and genetics. This does not mean that environmental factors can not affect the severity of the disorder, and in particular the extent to which the damage and suffering the child may be experiencing, but that these factors do not seem to be a condition by themselves.

The focus of the parents must be in the search of the best possible way to help the child. Researchers are studying causes in an effort to identify better ways to treat, and perhaps one day, to prevent this disorder. There has been evidence found proving that ADHD does not stem from the home environment, but that ADHD is due to biological reasons. Knowing this can remove a huge burden of guilt from parents who may be blaming themselves for their child's condition. In recent decades, researchers have proposed possible theories about ADHD causes. Some of these theories have led to dead ends, while others to exciting new avenues of research.

First off is the relationship of environmental agents and ADHD. Studies have shown a potential link between cigarette smoking and alcohol use during pregnancy, and the risk of ADHD in the offspring. As a precautionary measure, it is best to abstain from both cigarette and alcohol during pregnancy. Another agent in the environment, which may be related with a higher risk of ADHD, is high levels of lead in the bodies of young preschool children. Because lead is no longer allowed in paint and is found only in older buildings, exposure to toxic levels is not as widespread as it once was. Children living in older buildings where lead is still present in the paint or lead plumbing which has been painted may be at risk.

The relationship between ADHD and genetics has been perpetually discussed. Attention disorders often run in families, so it is likely that genetic influences are the cause of ADHD. Studies show that 25 percent of close relatives in the families of children with ADHD also have ADHD, while the rate is around 5 percent in the general population. Researchers continuously study the genetic contribution of ADHD, identifying genes that cause a person to be susceptible with ADHD.

The next suspected ADHD cause is brain injury. One theory is that the problems of attention disorders are caused by brain damage caused by trauma or injury. Some children who have had accidents resulting to brain injury may show signs of behavior similar to ADHD, but only a small percentage of children with ADHD were found to have suffered a head injury.

Lastly, food additives and sugar are thought to cause ADHD. It has been suggested that ADHD symptoms are caused by refined sugar or food additives, or the symptoms may cause exacerbation of the symptoms. It was found that diet restrictions aided those with ADHD, especially young children who have food allergies. However, recent studies on the effect of sugar on children, the use of sugar a day and a sugar substitute on alternate days, without parents, staff or children knowing which substance was used, showed no significant effect of sugar on behavior or learning.

Chapter 12: Parenting Adhd Children

Parenting is not an easy job. Most parents are pretty good at that but if your child suffers from ADHD, it could seem like an overwhelming job. As a parent it is important to remember that children with ADHD can and will succeed and shower them with unconditional love and support.

To ensure that your child grows up in a tranquil home environment, you need to guide your child in overcoming the challenges and channel-ize energy in a positive way so he/she reaches his potential and succeeds in life. It is important to understand the mindset of children and help them in overcoming resentment or dissatisfaction that might build up due to ADHD diagnosis. Parents and youngsters might need specialized guidance to assist their children in overcoming such feelings.

Parents could take up assistance of therapists to better understand ADHD and how their family is affected. Therapists can guide the parents and children into dealing with situations in a better way and create new mindsets and methods for understanding each other.

Certain changes in parenting styles and making adjustments can help the child adjust better. Instead of punishments or criticizing kids parents need to be on the lookout for good behaviour and reward them. Dealing with such situations is better if deal proactively than reactively. Positive reinforcements like a smile, positive inputs, praising or giving rewards for appropriate behaviour can go a long way in improving the attention, concentration and impulse control of such children.

While inappropriate behaviour should be handled with either overlooking or redirecting practices or giving time- out to let the child cool off. Constant criticism can erode the self-esteem of a child while praises and rewards can help them succeed in the long run.

Parents should accept their child has ADHD and encourage them in doing what they like to do well. Their good qualities and capabilities should be praised and help them in structuring circumstances in a positive way. If a child has difficulty finishing an assignment, it can be broken down into smaller tasks and encouraged into finishing small tasks. Often the entire family might require treatment; advisors can help families discover better approaches to handle inappropriate behaviour and conduct changes.

Support networks help families in coping with issues and concerns and discuss prescribed procedures and conversing with specialists. For most people, medicines and therapy works well. Counselling and therapies can be taken either individually, with family or group therapy usually helps in understanding and learning coping skills.

Family counselling helps in keeping parents informed and teaches them ways to help out kids with ADHD. It also improves communication within family and solves problems. Individual Counselling help in making the person understand his / her actions and learn coping skills whereas group therapy can help people with ADHD work on coping skills, learn from others and improving their social skills. Nowadays schools also come up with their own plans to help students learn in a manner best suited for them.

The effect of having a child suffering from ADHD on the family can be quite crucial. Kids can show many troublesome behaviour that can upset family life such as disobeying parents and ignoring the guidelines, being occupied in tasks or beginning a task and forgetting about it, blurting out inappropriate things, doing humiliating things or being hyperactive and cause disruption in the house and doing things that might put them in danger.

In these kinds of situation, the siblings might feel jealous or hatred as their needs might get less consideration, their achievements might be underestimated and they might be blamed if their sibling gets into mischief under their care and they can be scolded more if they make mistakes.

Parents also get affected as they need to take care of the child as the demands of children can be physically and psychologically exhausting. The child's inability to listen is frustrating and it can cause anger, frustration, stress and eventually guilt for being angry at your child. Parents must be able to deal with such situations with compassion and consistency. The best thing for a child learning to manage this disorder is to be in a loving and peaceful environment.

Following a fixed pattern and routine helps children cope in a better way. Unpredictable situations can be ambiguous for such kids and they might not perform daily activities properly if there's a surprise element for them. Hence, it is better to follow specific schedules for meals, homework, play and bed time and setting up clothes and other items in a fixed place which are to be taken to school, using clocks and timers possibly to set up time for homework, playing, nap times etc.

Parents must also accommodate the schedule in such a way that they don't have idle time as it may create distractions and it fits all the after school activities. It is important to have a quiet and private space for children as well as teach them to be neat and organized.

Children with ADHD are bustling with a lot of energy. Sports and physical activities give them the outlet to use this energy in a healthy way and make them focus on specific skills improving concentration. Physical activities help in improving concentration; help in decreasing depression, anxiety and also promote brain growth. It is also a well-known fact that exercise leads to a better sleep. A better sleep will help in reducing the symptoms. Sports like basketball, hockey, football that require constant motion are better options than probably chess or softball. Parents must find out the strengths and weakness and encourage their child to focus on activities suiting his or her strengths. Activities like martial arts, yoga and jujutsu enhance mental control and are good options for such kids.

Sleeping proper hours can also help in reduction of ADHD symptoms. Insufficient sleep can be adverse for children, they need as much sleep as children of their age but they don't tend to sleep as much. Inattention problem can cause over-stimulation and insomnia at times. Though early bedtime can be helpful but it may not completely solve the problem. Parents need to follow strategies like decreasing the television time, increasing activity and exercise level, eliminating caffeine from diet, finding quiet activities like reading to lower down activity level before bedtime, using relaxation tapes or spending time in nature.

Chapter 13: The Benefits Of Adhd

Attention hyperactivity disorder (ADHD) is a medical condition that affects a person's ability to focus, pay attention, or control their behavior. Healthcare providers usually diagnose this condition in childhood. However, some people are not diagnosed until adulthood.

The three main characteristics of a person with ADHD are inattention, hyperactivity, and impulsivity. ADHD also can cause a person to experience very high energy levels. Some symptoms associated with ADHD include:

being highly impatient

difficulty performing tasks quietly

difficulty following instructions

trouble waiting for things or showing patience

losing things frequently

often seeming as if they aren't paying attention

talking seemingly nonstop

There is no definitive test to diagnose ADHD. However, healthcare providers can evaluate children or adults for the condition based on symptoms. A number of treatments are available to improve a person's concentration and behavior. These include medications and therapy. ADHD is a highly manageable disease. When taught adaptive techniques to help with time management and organization skills, people with ADHD are able to achieve better levels of concentration.

ADHD can be difficult for a person to live with. Some people think those with ADHD are "out of control" or difficult because they have trouble following directions. While ADHD can mean behavioral challenges, having the condition has proven to be an advantage to some.

Personality Strengths and ADHD

Not every person with ADHD has the same personality traits, but there are some personal strengths that can make having the condition an advantage, not a drawback. Examples of these traits include:

energetic: Some with ADHD often have seemingly endless amounts of energy, which they are able to channel toward success on the playing field, school, or work.

spontaneous: Some people with ADHD can turn impulsivity into spontaneity. They may be the life of the party or may be more open and willing to try new things and break free from the status quo.

creative and inventive: Living with ADHD may give the person a different perspective on life and encourage them to approach tasks and situations with a thoughtful eye. As a result, some with ADHD may be inventive thinkers. Others words to describe them may be original, artistic, and creative.

hyperfocused: According to Pepperdine University, some people with ADHD may become hyperfocused. This makes them so intently focused on a task that they may not even notice the world around them.

The benefit to this is when given an assignment, a person with ADHD may work at it until its completion without breaking concentration.

Common Misconceptions About ADHD

These five myths about ADHD need to go now.

As is unfortunately the case with many other health conditions, there are numerous misconceptions that surround ADHD. These misunderstandings about the condition are harmful to the folks within the community. They can result in problems such as delays in diagnosis and accessing treatment, not to mention leaving people feeling misunderstood.

Take my patient Vanessa. She spent years struggling at school, both in high school and college. During those years, she was unable to retain information she had spent hours learning and constantly felt anxious at the thought of the things she had to do.

It wasn't until she sought the help of a psychiatrist while at college and was diagnosed with ADHD that she understood why this was happening to her. Had Vanessa been diagnosed at an earlier age, she may have been given the appropriate tools to help her through school.

According to the National Alliance of Mental Illness (NAMI), about 9 percent of children have ADHD, while around 4 percent of adults have it. Chances are you know someone with the condition. In light of May being Mental Health Awareness month, I've pulled together five myths about ADHD that need dispelling now, in hopes of shedding light on the reality of this condition.

Myth 1: Girls don't get ADHD

In general, young girls aren't as likely to be as hyperactive as young boys or display as many behavioral issues compared to boys, so people often don't recognize ADHD in girls.

As a result, girls are less likelyTrusted Source to be referred for an evaluation of ADHD. The problem with this myth is that, because girls with ADHD often go untreated, their condition can progress, increasing issues with:

mood

anxiety

antisocial personality

other comorbid disorders in adulthood

It's for this reason that it's really important to improve our ability to identify girls with ADHD and provide them with the support they need.

Myth 2: Poor parenting causes ADHD

Some of my adult patients with ADHD will bring their parents into their appointments. During these sessions, I often find that the parents will share their guilt of wishing they could've done more to help their kid succeed and control their symptoms.

This often stems from the myth that "poor parenting" causes ADHD. But the fact is, this is not the case. Though structure is important for a person with ADHD, constant punishing for symptoms such as blurting out words, restlessness, hyperactivity, or impulsivity can be more detrimental in the long run.

But because many would view this type of behavior as the child simply being "poorly mannered," parents often find themselves being judged for not being able to control their child. This is why professional interventions such as psychotherapy and medications are often required.

Myth 3: People with ADHD are lazy

Many of my patients with ADHD explain that they're often accused of being lazy, which leaves them feeling guilty for not being as productive and motivated as others expect them to be.

Folks with ADHD tend to need more structure and reminders to get things done especially activities that require sustained mental effort. But because symptoms of ADHD may manifest as disinterest, disorganization, and a lack of motivation unless it's related to an activity they truly enjoy, this may be mistaken for laziness.

However, the reality is that people with ADHD truly want to succeed but may struggle to initiate and complete what others may consider "simple" tasks.

Even sorting through mail or answering an email can be daunting because it requires a lot more sustained mental energy for someone with this condition. This myth can be especially harmful as these judgments can leave people with a sense of failure, which can progress to poor self-esteem and lacking confidence to pursue ventures in life.

Myth 4: Having ADHD 'isn't that serious'

While ADHD isn't life-threatening, it can have serious implications on a person's overall quality of life. Compared to the general population, people with ADHD are more likely to have:

anxiety

mood and substance use disorders

Meanwhile, one common experience among my patients with ADHD is that it's difficult to keep up with work responsibilities, and they're constantly monitored or on probation.

This means they live in continual fear of losing their jobs and not being able to keep up financially, which can take a toll on their personal life.

Folks with ADHD may require more time to complete tasks in order to thrive. Unfortunately, while these sorts of accommodations may be available in educational settings think longer test-taking time or quiet exam rooms employers may not be as willing to accommodate.

Myth 5: ADHD isn't a real medical disorder

Research has demonstrated differences between a brain with ADHD and one without it, in addition to differences in how brain chemicals such as dopamine, norepinephrine, and glutamate operate. The parts of the brain involved in ADHD play an important part in our "executive functions," such as:

planning

organizing

initiating tasks

Twin studies also suggest that ADHD has a genetic component, where in identical twins, if one twin has ADHD, the other is likely to have it as well.

The bottom line

As it stands, individuals with ADHD are often judged and unfairly labelled. Moreover, they often find:

accommodations aren't made in order for them to be successful

they aren't diagnosed early enough

they come up against those in society who don't believe ADHD is even a condition

For these reasons and more, the myths that surround ADHD need dispelling if we're to raise awareness about this condition and provide folks within the community with what they need to succeed in all aspects of their lives.

Chapter 14: Attention Deficit Disorder: Is It Really That?

Attention Deficit Disorder or ADD is most frequently identified in boys of primary school age. Indications consist of lack of concentration, being restless, reckless mannerisms, or lack of focus. But what brings about these indications, in fact? And should every one of the occurrences of ADD be treated?

In a few occurrences, the indications of ADD may in fact be indicative of a more severe psychological predicament, such as depression, bipolar disorder, brain defects and even nervousness. On the other hand, at times the occurrence of the particular inattentive behavior may simply be due to allergic reactions, sensitivities to the environment, nutritional deficits or also too much caffeine.

Many times, young boys are wrongly diagnosed with Attention Deficit Disorder merely for conducting themselves the way anybody would be expecting. Young boys will by and large make reckless resolutions, have a lot of superfluous energy, cannot sit still, and have short concentration period in school. Combined with the fact that the majority of school age children use up more than forty hours a week watching TV and playing computer games, it is not a surprise that a lot of children have energy to use up.

ADD mannerism is frequently indicative of creativeness, giftedness, high aptitude, and a child being a visual theorist.

In short, an analysis of Attention Deficit Disorder ought to be thought of as a start, and not an end. Too frequently, when a doctor sees that a child is agitated and has a short concentration period, she writes a medication for Dexedrine or Ritalin and that is that. But these drugs have possibly unsafe side effects, and are not essentially going to cure the predicament at all.

A further comprehensive examination of the occurrence generally falls upon the child's parents. The facts stated here is aimed to steer the parents in the right track, giving propositions of where to begin looking for the reason of the child's Attention Deficit Disorder related manners.

Understanding And Treating ADHD

Attention Deficit Hyperactivity Disorder: What Is It?

Attention Deficit Hyperactivity Disorder or ADHD is a mental disorder, which approximately three to seven percent children are having. Due to this disorder children manifest the characteristic of constant behavior, loads of activity as well as often being considered disobedient. That does not mean that the individual is being bad but the thing is, they don't have control over their mental range. They go through lack of concentration because at a time they are likely to be thinking about many elements instead of one particular element.

This disorder is also found in many adults besides children. In adults, it is called Adult Attention Deficit Disorder or AADD. Among all children diagnosed with ADHD about 30 to 70 percent will carry on with their disorder through adulthood. Adults learn to live with it and work around it and need less help. They can handle the disorder of their own and so it's harder to detect also. Yet, in many cases both children and adult may need medications for better results.

In children this disorder shows signs like inattentiveness, impulsive behavior and a constant restlessness. In adults, it is harder to diagnose but children with this disorder cannot sit still for long. They cannot concentrate on one particular thing for a long period of time. In adults, it becomes difficult sometimes to structure their lives and to plan daily activities. They don't feel the importance to stay attentive or to stop being restless because these are not at all important problems for them.

ADHD is a disorder for which assistance of medical personnel is necessary. It can be treated but cannot be cured fully. For this disorder medication is also necessary.

Understanding And Treating ADHD

6 Tips For Slowing Down The ADD Brain

If you are an adult suffering with ADD, then you might recognize that although it is easy to say, slowing down can be a very difficult if not impossible thing to do at first glance.

No matter who you are there are numerous things that have to be done and all too often little time available to get them done. So then your mind starts to work at high speed in an attempt to achieve as much as it can and more. The result can be stress at not being able to meet your requirements, leading to you getting upset about the fact that it looks impossible. Because of this you use up lots of time worrying, and unfortunately little time enjoying yourself.

Whilst slowing down can be a complex thing to achieve it can be done. Here are six established methods to assist you to slow your brain ADD or otherwise:

1. Put down your work

Set business hours and no matter what is left at the end of the day, walk away. Stand by your rules. Even though it is going to seem necessary to work overtime, avoid it at all cost. You will work better and more efficiently during the shorter hours of the day knowing that you must leave at a set time. And take weekends (or at least a couple of days a week off).

2. Commit to a regular obligation

Commit to a reason to get out of your house or out of your office each week. You may want to attend a class, possibly something that you have always wanted to do. Make sure that you 'pay' in advance for the class so that you have a reason to attend.

3. Arrange for a break with others

Few things are as enjoyable as having a night out with friends. This may be with colleagues, with friends, with family, or with members of another group.

Understanding And Treating ADHD

4. Keep a diary

Writing in a diary requires that you stop, think about what you want to say, and then act on what you think. It helps you to deal with nervous tension and achieve clearness. make a resolution to write every day - even if only for a few minutes!

5. Switch your computer off two hours before bed

Because computers are an access point to interesting things, for ADDers you can find yourself sitting at a computer until the early hours of the morning completely oblivious to what is happening around you. To make sure that this doesn't happen to you switch the computer off at least 2 hours before you plan to go to sleep so as to suitably relax and slow down at night.

6. Meditate

There are diverse methods of meditation, so find one that suits you, but you may want to consider mindfulness meditation. This is the action of keeping your mind in the present - whether you are walking, working or washing dishes. Make an effort to keep your mind in the here and now not the past or future.

It is fine to start doing this little by little, with short sessions spent in mindful meditation daily (possibly only 5 minutes at a time), after that building your performance as you become more at ease.

Chapter 15: Adult Suffers Of Adhd

Life can be challenging as an adult, but if you find yourself always being late to appointments or your job, seem disorganized and forgetful, and overwhelmed by your day to day responsibilities, you may have ADHD. Attention Deficit Hyperactivity Disorder affects many adults, which symptoms can affect everything from relationships to careers.

If you were diagnosed with ADHD as a child, chances are, you still have some of the symptoms of ADHD as an adult. Even if you were never diagnosed with ADHD as a child, you still can have ADHD as an adult.

ADHD can often go undiagnosed throughout childhood. This was especially common 30 years ago, when very few people were aware of what ADHD was. Instead of recognizing the symptoms, your family, teachers, or other parents may have thought of you as a day dreamer, a goof-off, a troublemaker, or just a lazy or bad student.

Signs and symptoms of adult ADHD

In adults, the signs and symptoms of ADHD are similar as they are in children, however they can look quite different. Adults with ADHD tend to hide or mask their symptoms more effectively than children. Adults with ADHD tend to have difficulty staying focused on daily, mundane tasks. For example, adults may be easily distracted by events or sounds around them, quickly switch from one activity to another, or give up on activities more quickly. Adult symptoms are sometimes overlooked because they are deemed as laziness or lack of desire.

Signs and Symptoms of adult inattentive ADHD

Zoning or spacing out, usually without even realizing it, sometimes even when they are in the middle of a conversation.

Is easily distracted.

Difficulty paying attention staying focused or completing tasks, even simple ones.

Difficulty reading or listening to others.

Unable to follow instructions, causing errors or incomplete work.

Difficulty in remembering and following directions.

Adults, just like children suffer another symptom of Inattentive ADHD, that can seem opposite of the normal symptom of not staying focused. It is called Hyperfocus. It is where one will seem locked on to a task, so much, that they seem unaware of anything else around them.

Hyperfocus, can be a beneficial symptom, as it can allow one to succeed. A perfect example, is Olympic swimmer, Michael Phelps. He is a diagnosed ADHD suffer, yet he uses hyperfocus to remain locked in while he works for hours to better himself in swimming. There are disadvantages to hyperfocus as well. A perfect example of this is someone hyperfocused while playing video games. They can literally play for hours on end, without having any concept of time. They can spend all night playing, then all the sudden, it is morning and they are late for work or school. As an adult, when you have ADHD, life often can seem out of control. Remaining focused and organized can be a challenge.

Common signs of being disorganized

poor organizational skills, home or office is always cluttered

tendency to procrastinate, even with simple tasks

trouble starting and finishing activities

always is late for work, meetings, appointments and deadlines

constantly loses belongings

cannot complete tasks in a timely manner

Many adults with ADHD have a hard time dealing with their feelings, especially with emotions such as anger. If you or a loved one are experiencing emotions that make you feel like you want to hurt yourself or others, seek help immediately.

Emotional signs and symptoms of adult ADHD

Feelings of underachievement

Always seems frustrated

Always seems stressed out

irritability

trouble remaining motivated

explosive, temper

little or no self-esteem

Hyperactivity in adults with ADHD can appear similar as it does in children. You may be highly energetic as if driven by a motor, seemingly always on the go. For many with ADHD, the symptoms of hyperactivity tend to become more subtle, especially as they get older.

Common symptoms of hyperactivity in adults

feeling agitated or restless

takes unnecessary risks

gets easily bored

racing thoughts

trouble sitting still

talking excessively

seems to be doing a million things at the same time

Common effects of adult ADHD

If you are just now discovering, or have recently been diagnosed with adult ADHD, chances are you've been suffering with ADHD for many years. Most likely, you have been labeled as "lazy" or "stupid" because you always seem to forget things, or you have difficulty completing activities or tasks.

Undiagnosed ADHD can affect virtually every aspect of your adult life. It can cause or contribute to many health problems such as compulsive eating, alcohol or substance abuse, anxiety, stress, and low self-esteem. Suffers tend to also neglect their own health and miss important doctor appointments or check-ups, forgetting to take medications, or not paying attention to important medical information.

ADHD can affect your career. You may find yourself having difficulty in keeping a job, follow rules, meeting deadlines, or keeping to a routine. Having relationships with your peers can also be challenging in the employment area. You may feel inadequate, have no confidence in your abilities or feel like all eyes are on you.

Personal relationships can also suffer, just as with professional relationships. The most important factor is ensuring loved ones know what ADHD is and is about, so they can understand and help the sufferer cope and deal with the condition.

Treatments for adult ADHD are basically the same as with children.

Common treatments for adult ADHD

Medications

Exercise

Healthy eating

Sleep and rest

Relationship counseling

Develop work organization skills

Seek mental health treatment and counselling

Chapter 16: What Is Add / Adhd?

I will start by explaining the abbreviations ADHD and ADD. The term ADHD is English and is an abbreviation for Attention Deficit Hyperactivity Disorder. People who have been diagnosed with ADD as opposed to those with ADHD are not hyperactive. Therefore, the description ADD is the abbreviation of Attention Deficit Disorder.

The history of ADHD.

Previously it was believed that only children had ADHD, and it usually disappeared in adulthood. As a rule, only those who were hyperactive where discovered when they made themselves noticed by "climbing walls." Those who had, what we today call ADD, did not draw attention to themselves and were therefore not seen as problematic. It had also been observed that those who had ADHD as children were quieter as adults. This has subsequently been proved to be due to the outer restlessness one had as a child, being turned inward when adult. The chaos was still there, but the adults were now able to hide it. This observation was precisely used to substantiate the claim that it was only children who could have ADHD, and the disorder disappeared when one were an adult.

Today we know better. We have become better at diagnosing adults with ADHD and ADD. But there is still a long way to go. There is at present no way to physically measure ADHD. Nowadays, you would have to consult a psychiatrist. You would then typically fill in questionnaires, which in turn are analysed by the psychiatrist.

ADHD was first formally recognized as a medical disorder by the American Psychiatric Association in the late 60s. This especially can be an important factor in explaining the explosive increase of ADHD diagnoses since the 1990s. The number of people with these disorders / difficulties may always have been the same. But we're just getting better at diagnosing it. Some even believe that we have only seen the tip of the iceberg. You can compare it to the time when one did not yet know what appendicitis was. Before the diagnosis was recognized, people just had stomach-ache, and eventually died from it. But when it was discovered what caused it, the statistics rose as doctors became better at diagnosing appendicitis.

ADD the quiet ADHD

Since ADD is the quiet type of ADHD, it is often still very hard to find us who have ADD. Typically, we are able to go "under the radar" and we develop survival strategies which means we are still doing fairly well throughout life. Typically, it first surfaces when you get into a relationship, and when you start to have children. One is pressured on a whole different level, and the coping skills that have been built up begin to collapse. There are also many adults who first find out that they have the disorder when their children are diagnosed with either ADHD or ADD. They recognize their children's patterns in themselves and begin to see the connection between their own childhood and the explanations and findings in the children's diagnosis.

ADHD and ADD are basically the same. The only difference is that a person with ADHD have an outwardly unrest in the body with many movements where a person with ADD have inward unrest. Both people find it very hard to concentrate.

In my own case, my wife was on the verge of leaving me when she was pregnant with our first son. I could not keep appointments, and I never arrived on time. Overall, I was never to be trusted. I felt pushed into a corner. I could see the actual situations where I failed. But I had no way of finding a pattern in why I failed. I remember the time when I was late for the first midwife consultation. We had agreed that we would meet after work, down by the midwife at a specific time. I had calculated that it would take 30 minutes to drive from work until the car was parked in front of the midwife's office. But there were a few things that I just had to finish first. I thought that I would arrive on time if I just pressed a little more on the accelerator. What I had not counted on was that it also takes 10 minutes to turn off my PC, 5 minutes to pack my bag and go out to the car, the traffic, and that we had actually agreed that I should pick up my wife at home first and would not meet at the midwifes. When I was almost home, she sent a text message which said that she had cycled down (pregnant in a snowstorm) and was waiting for me in the midwife's consulting room. That afternoon I sat in our hallway and cried. I did not have a clue what to do. What was wrong with me! And why could I not get a grip on myself? There was no rhyme or reason to the mistakes I made. I had no idea where to start to get better. When my wife talked to a friend about this incident she thought that I might have ADHD. I had never heard of ADHD, but I was willing to do anything to save our relationship. We got an appointment with my doctor so that he could judge whether I should be referred to a psychiatrist. Even that was a challenge. The doctor thought initially that there could be no question about ADHD. Since I had been able to qualify as a software engineer, it could not be ADHD. It has to be mentioned that my apprenticeship required enormous amounts of effort on my part, and that I could never quite understand how my classmates were able to deliver so much more than me. But fortunately I had my wife with me, a qualified pedagogue who has worked extensively with children with ADHD. She explained to him the difficulties that she had observed I was battling with. He agreed to give me a referral to a psychiatrist. For which I am today deeply grateful. Now I had something concrete I could grasp. I had something I could work with.

The brain's neurotransmitters

When you have ADHD there is an imbalance in the brain's neurotransmitters. When people learn something new or succeed with something, a chemical is secreted a in the brain called dopamine. This substance is picked up by some receptors which results in a form of happiness. When you learn something new, which require long-term concentration, you are able to keep the concentration because the sub consciousness know that when you succeed, there will be a reward. This is what we call the brain's reward system. This system is precisely the reason why we humans are able to develop. When having ADHD, there is an imbalance in this system. Consequently one does not have the same natural motivation or impetus to stay focused over longer periods.

Because of this imbalance of the reward system, some people with ADHD do not get the proper batch of dopamine. This affects that some may also find it hard to stay away from unhealthy things. This could be anything from the innocent sweets, to alcohol or drugs. It is often seen that people with ADHD smoke cigarettes, have an alcohol or drug abuse problem. These substances is able to provide the brain with neurotransmitters which the brain lacks.

Chapter 17: The Role Of Omega-3 Fatty Acids

Another important key in nutritional therapy is adding the right supplements.

Studies have shown that omega-3 fatty acid helps anyone to improve focus, but it can be especially useful for people suffering from ADHD.

Omega-3 can be found in many tasty foods like wild rice, walnuts, canola oil, beans, seafood and, especially fish. Salmon and sardines are rich in this compound. The human body can't create it so eating the right foods will help, but that may not be enough so, you may want to consider adding a supplement in your child diet. Children would greatly benefit from ingesting 2.5 grams of fish oil every day. There are no side effects and the improvements don't reflect just on the behavioral aspects. Omega-3 is used to reduce the risk of obesity, prevent cancer, improve the overall aspect of hair and nails, minimize the risk of cardiovascular disease, and the list could go on.

The role of physical activity in improving ADHD symptoms

If we were to look for the human behavior that changed most with evolution, it would definitely be our approach to physical activity.

Humans are designed to run for survival, to hunt in open air, to climb trees for healthy food, and to sleep at night.

Although, people may think this happened back when cave men roamed the Earth, the truth is that, it has been happening for thousands of years, and only in the past hungered years or so, did we changed our ways. This means that our bodies haven't had the time to adapt.

You are probably wandering why we are talking about physical activity when the main subject is a cognitive condition.

When engaged in any kind of sports, be it running, swimming, playing ball or doing a set of pushups, our body releases chemicals, and among those chemicals there is endorphin. Endorphin is a hormone-like chemical that can regulate mood and pleasure.

Also, any physical activity will increase the amount of dopamine and serotonin which, we already know, are found in low levels in those with ADHD.

Half an hour of exercise a day, will help any child's focus, and diminish the impulsive tendencies. This may sound too simple to be true, but studies have shown that sport has a positive influence in children suffering from ADHD. Even if simply running in the park four times a week would help, research shows that activities like mountain biking, skateboarding, ballet, martial arts, swimming and gymnastics are especially good for children, and adults, suffering from ADHD.

This happens because the movement, that these kinds of sports involve, is a bit more complex, and requires coordination, and they activate parts of the brain that control balance, sequencing, error correction and motor adjustments, leading to intense focus and concentration.

The approach to sport shouldn't be just physical and biochemical. It is a known fact that exercise helps dealing with past failures and increases self-confidence. Many children with ADHD feel helpless and think that they will fail at anything they try, but when introduced to a specific sport that appeals them, they improve their emotional balance and they are always pleasantly surprised by the outcome.

Most kids would love the idea of taking part in any sport but, there are those that hate any type of physical activity so, it's the parent's role to find the kind of sport that is enjoyable. It might seem hard in the beginning, but in time it will definitely become more than pleasant, and not only will your child's behavior improve, but also there overall health.

Behavioral Therapy

Behavioral Therapy sounds like something extremely complicated, and possibly like a notion taken from a sci-fi novel. The fact is that it's quite simple and pleasant.

It is based on the idea that bad behaviors are not based on a person's character, but rather on how learning influences their reaction in certain situations.

The ground rules of this kind of therapy were set down a long time ago by Ivan Pavlov. And, as I stated before it's not as bad as it sounds. It focuses on giving a person a single task, and giving an immediate reward, once the task is complete.

The tricky part for parents is having just a single task for their children. The main point is to develop specific rules. When the rule is fallowed there will be positive consequences. If the rule isn't fallowed there will be negative consequences.

Right now you are probably thinking that you have done this all the time, and you probably have, but the approach is a bit different.

How to use behavioral therapy

First of all, you must choose a single goal in order to observe progress. The goal shouldn't be divided into many others, because that would overwhelm the child and you won't be able to see the results. If you want your child to eat all the veggies, stay still during dinner, and wash the plates that may be too much. Choose just one and stick with it. Baby steps are the key here.

Second of all, you must make a chart, a table of rules in which to write down what you expect your child to do, and what he can get out of it. Put this chart in a very visible spot. You can make it fun by using colors, by asking your kid what else to put in, getting him or her involved will make the rules easier to follow, especially if you make it seem like it was his idea in the first place.

The third step is probably the most important. You must reward your child very fast, and with enthusiasm every time he does the right thing. Even for the small things that seem irrelevant. You can write it down on the chart as a prize, and tell the other members of your family how good he's been. Speak proudly about his success and give him what you promised he'd get, maybe extra TV time or whatever you decided.

If he fails to respect the rule, there must be consequences, but nothing to drastic and it should also be immediate. Take away privileges, and put it on the chart.

So, you've noticed that there is no big deal in this "behavioral therapy", the basics are simple, probably too simple, but research showed that it is very effective, and it can bring huge benefits to a child with behavior issues.

Chapter 18: Where Does My Child Shine?

By now you should have a pretty good understanding of which executive skills your child lacks in as well as how your own weaknesses and perceptions can affect their growth. It is inevitable that there will be times when your own strengths will pull against your child's weaknesses and vice versa. There will be times when the two of you can work together because you are both strong in a certain skill set, but there will also be times when your weaknesses will come up against your child's strong point. Still, the worst case scenario is to have to overcome a skill that both of you are weak in.

As you can probably see by now, there will be many challenges yet to face, but in spite of them all, you never want to lose sight of your ultimate goal. How to help your child to shine in this world. One of the first and probably most important steps to accomplishing this goal is to learn everything you can about your child.

When you can identify which executive skills he is weak in then, you will be able to lay out a specific plan of action that the two of you can work at together. Simply by doing this, you will begin to see just how to tap into your child's strong points in order to carve out a path that will give him what he needs.

It is sometimes said, "Whenever the door is locked, try a window." The child with ADHD may have to climb through the window in order to achieve his goal, unlike other children who could simply walk through the door. In other words, they may have to find alternative methods for achieving the same goal because of their lack of executive skills.

This will require you to be observant not just of your child and your family dynamics but also the interactions he has throughout the day. If a task is assigned that does not fit well into one of his stronger executive skills, then you may have to find an alternative approach to accomplish the goal. Each time your child is successful, his self-esteem will grow, and he will be more eager to try again.

Many parents hold to the idea that self-esteem comes from showering their child with compliments and praise and while that is warranted at times there is another, more effective way of building self-esteem in the child. By helping them to succeed on their own. Whenever the child is presented with a task that will challenge their limited ability to execute, showing them how to find an alternative approach to the task could do wonders in how they feel about themselves. When they can accomplish the task to the end, they will be more eager to try again the next time a task is expected of them.

This is not always easy to do. At times, you will recognize immediately that the task is not the right match for your child's skills but at other times it may not be so simple. Learn your child's level of tolerance and be proactive in deciding beforehand whenever possible which activities your child has the best chance to succeed in.

Those that you know they can't accomplish try to establish an alternative plan of action to ensure that they are successful.

Managing the School Environment

School is one of those situations where it may not be easy for the parent to suggest alternative assignments or for children to get out of doing certain activities. Helping your child to develop flexibility and emotional control can go a long way in getting them to plow through the task they have in front of them. After all, school is specifically designed to prepare the child for life, and very few things in life will be adjusted to one's liking. In these cases, parents and children together will need to develop a strategy to help them adapt to the situation.

To do this, there are several factors the parents must keep in mind.

When an assignment requires your child to tap into their own weaknesses in a particular executive skill, it is important that you pay close attention to their emotional state of mind.

It is very important that the parent tries to understand the reason for the emotional change. When a child has a tantrum, avoid thinking it is just an act of rebellion and try to find out the underlying cause. Children tend to behave very differently at home than they do at school when they are surrounded by their peers. They may be too embarrassed to speak up at school, but if you have an open channel of communication, it may be easier for them to let you know what's bothering them.

It has been said by some parents, "The child that needs love the most tends to ask for it in the most unloving of ways." They may not know how to express themselves clearly so you may have to read between the lines, but once you know the root cause of the emotional behavior the better equipped, you'll be to manage the situation and direct the child accordingly.

2. When they appear to be avoiding an assignment or chore, don't conclude they

129

are being lazy or rebellious. They just may not be able to do it.

Children react to situations in different ways and may not always be able to say they can't do something. Some may lash out in anger, others may withdraw into themselves, and others may simply procrastinate and never get started on the task. These are common tactics that are there to let you know there is a problem.

It is the parent's responsibility to look at the task and try to identify which executive skills are needed and why the child is struggling with it. Then you must create a plan of action that will help the child to address the issue.

3. Look at each task and try to decide which executive skills are needed and decide if your child has developed them.

By understanding the task and the executive skills required, you can compare it to your child's weaknesses and strengths. When an assignment requires a number of skills to complete you can try to find the point at which the child breaks the flow. For example, if the assignment is to write an essay for school, go down the list and see which of your child's weak skills is interrupting the work. Is it at the planning stage or at the emotional stage? Is their weakness in metacognition or is it with flexibility?

4. Determine if the difficulty is in the child or is it from the environment.

Sometimes the problem is not in the assignment but in the environment. TV or music playing in the background could add unnecessary distractions that prevent the child from staying on point; other children may be self-conscious and not able to focus if they are being watched too closely. Some children may require close observation where others may want independence to work on their own. Only you know your child and their strengths and weaknesses.

5. The Sometimey Child

There are those children that can perform a task in one environment while placing them in another environment renders them incapable of functioning. This may be challenging for a parent, teacher, or child to recognize. The child may have mastered the assignment and knows how to do it well, but the challenge comes when the child has to do it repeatedly.

These situations may be organizational where they must clean up their room or maintain a specific record. As the parent, you may have to make some decisions to ensure that you maintain control over the situation. You may choose to monitor the child regularly to make sure that they channel their energies in the right direction or you might opt to allow the child to slip out of the mode for a while and then go back to it. How you manage, it will depend largely on which emotional skills they are struggling with.

6. Find out What Happens When the Child Succeeds

If they are struggling with a task they have successfully completed before then you need to go back and look at what was different. Did you give them more encouragement? Was the environment conducive to what they need to focus? Was the assignment more difficult, shorter, harder, more interesting? Was it broken down into smaller easier to manage pieces? Did they have breaks? There could be a wide number of factors that can interfere with their progress on a particular task. If they have succeeded before then you know, they can do it, so it has to be something else that is triggering the break.

7. Does the child believe in himself?

Sometimes they have the skills needed to perform the task, but for some reason, they don't believe they can do it. There could be a number of things that can strip a child of self-confidence; they think the task is too big; they had tried the same thing before and failed; they have been criticized or bullied, or someone may have tried to help by taking over the job themselves. Whatever the case may be, helping to build up their self-esteem can boost their spirit in amazing ways.

All of this translates into one simple thought. Being a parent of an ADHD child is hard work but if you want to help your child shine in a way that they can be proud of the rewards on the other side can be amazing.

Chapter 19: Encourage Your Child To Make Friends, Move Right, And Sleep On Time

Encouraging a child with ADHD to make friends, move right, and sleep on time can help a lot in turning him or her into a better person. The main focus here is to encourage even though there might be times when everything seems too impossible to make.

Encourage your Child with ADHD to Make Friends

Children with ADHD often find it hard to establish social interactions. They may struggle finding the right social cues; they tend to interrupt almost every now and then, too talkative, or leave an impression that can be considered as too intense. The emotional immaturities that they possess make them standout, and that made them an easy target of other kids to tease.

Bear in mind that many children with ADHD are remarkably creative and intelligent. They will be able to figure out sooner or later how to deal with others, and recognize who they should be friends with.

Helping the Child Develop Social Skills.

Children with ADHD find it difficult to understand social skills and the rules that should be followed. You can help the child to interact with finesse while in a group, be a better listener, and learn to read body language and faces of people.

You can start by speaking softly to your child and with all honesty. Tell him or her about possible challenges that might be faced, and how to bring about change.

Role-play different social scenes with your child. Assign and assume a particular role to illustrate it better. Trade roles and make him or her understand the feeling and thoughts of a particular character, and don't forget to always incorporate the element of fun.

When ready, select a playmate for your child and to be on the safe side, pick a relative (a cousin) who is about the same age as your child. Watch everything closely while they play and take note of the areas that your child needs to improve.

Establish a zero tolerance policy for yelling, hitting, and / or pushing while in your premises. Allow your child to play, and offer a reward for behaving well.

Moving Right

Physical activity can help a child with ADHD a lot. Children with such condition often have much energy to burn. Organize sporting events and other activities that will make them make use of their energy in a good way, and focus their attention on a particular skill and movement.

Physical activity improves your child's concentration, allows fresh neurons to develop, and diminishes anxiety and depression. Exercise can make your child sleep better, which can help reduce symptoms of ADHD.

Discover the activity that your child enjoys most and encourage him or her to continue pursuing the activity.

Better Sleep Means Less Symptoms

Children with ADHD have trouble falling asleep because their attention problems often lead to overstimulation that makes it hard for them to fall asleep. Letting your child go to bed earlier might help combat the problem, but it does not guarantee that this is the best solution.

You can try to decrease the time your child spent watching TV and increase the activities during the day.

You can also lower down the activity level at least an hour or so before sending your child to bed. You can do simple coloring, story telling, reading, or quiet playing.

Cuddling can help ease your child, so make sure to spend some time cuddling him or her.

Use relaxing sounds as your background while you try to put your child to sleep. You can also add an aromatic lavender scent to fill the room, and try massaging your child gently to relax his or her body.

Do all of these and you will surely see some improvements in the days to come.

Chapter 20: Natural And Alternative Remedies

In addition to setting a specific treatment plan for your child, consider trying some of the home remedies listed in this chapter. The more tools your child has, the better he can combat his condition. The following remedies have been researched and deemed safe for children with ADHD:

Avoid food colorings: While research regarding the harmful effects of food colorings and preservatives is inconclusive, it wouldn't hurt to give it the benefit of the doubt. Some studies have shown that certain food colorings may actually increase hyperactivity. When feeding your child store-bought food, read the labels thoroughly. Avoid the following food colorings and preservatives as much as possible:

Sodium benzoate

Red No. 40

Yellow No. 5

Yellow No. 6

Yellow No. 10

2. **Restrict potential allergens:** Avoiding possible allergens can go a long in approving the behavior of a child who has ADHD. While it's best to talk to your child's doctor if you suspect he has allergies, you can try experimenting by avoiding the following foods:

Food additives like BHT and BHA, which are found in potato chips, instant mashed potatoes and grits, chewing gum, and some cereals.

Foods that contain salicylates, including plums, peaches, prunes, and tomatoes.

Dairy products like milk and eggs.

Chocolate

Soy products

Peanuts

Shellfish

3. **Considering trying EEG biofeedback:** EEG biofeedback is a learning strategy designed to teach a person to control his or her brainwaves. In other words, EEG biofeedback is an exercise for your child's brain which allows him to retrain his brain. EEG biofeedback may involve having your child play video games while he is hooked up to a monitor. The machine will then measure his brainwave activity and his reactions to the game, as well as the strategies he uses to win the game. By providing your child with information regarding his own unique brainwaves, he can then be taught techniques for learning how to control his brainwaves. Research is currently underway that explores the potential of EEG biofeedback to permanently cure ADHD.

4. **Try massage therapy:** Massage has a positive effect on children suffering from ADHD. It improves mood and reduces

hyperactivity. Just two 20-minute massage therapy sessions each week has the power to improve ADHD symptoms.

5. **Meditative and relaxation activities:** Try meditating with your child for 5-10 minutes every day. Meditation is a simple practice to take up. Having your child focus on nothing but his breaths for a few minutes will calm both a hyperactive and impulsive brain. Alternatively, you can use guided imagery as a relaxation exercise. Guided imagery used words, images, or music to focus and direct the imagination. If you have a teenage child with ADHD, Yoga and Tai Chi can provide a sense of discipline and improve symptoms.

6. **Use mirrors:** Placing a mirror in front of your child while he works on completing a task may help keep him focused and keep him from getting off track. However, it will only work if your child is aware of his condition.

7. **Brahmi:** Also known as water hyssop, brahmi is a medicinal plant that is native to India. Brahmi has been used in both

ancient and modern health practices to improve brain function, increase intelligence, and sharpen memory. In fact, brahmi is one of the most commonly recommended herb for complementing traditional ADHD treatment plans. Brahmi is available as a powder, syrup, or as it is.

8. **Gotu kola:** This plant is known to stimulate the nervous system, thus helping ADHD patients experience mental clarity. It has a high concentration of nutrients that are vital for healthy brain function. Gotu kola also affects the production of neurotransmitter, or chemicals in the brain. Gotu kola works best when used in combination with ginkgo biloba when dealing with learning disabilities and ADHD. In children with ADHD, gotu kola works by heightening mental function and enhancing learning capabilities.

9. **Ginseng:** Having your child drink ginseng tea will improve his sleep habits and boost his memory. Siberian ginseng, in particular, is well-regarded for increasing mental stamina. If your child does not like

the taste of ginseng, try sweetening the tea with a teaspoon of honey.

10. **Wild oats:** Comparable to oatmeal, wild oats are highly nutritious and chock full of the minerals that are essential for a healthy nervous system such as iron and magnesium. If anxiety or tension is an issue with your child, wild oats can help. You can wild oats a breakfast staple in your home by substituting oatmeal for wild oats. Prepare wild oats like you would oatmeal, and serve it with cinnamon and a drizzle of honey. Your child may not even notice the difference! Alternatively, you can incorporate wild oats in granola and oatmeal raisin cookies.

11. **Vervain:** Vervain is an effective relaxant for the nervous system. It is most commonly used in cases of hyperactivity in children. The vervain herb helps manage blood pressure, and has a restorative effect on the nervous systems. When the effects of vervain are combined, the herb has the power of curbing hyperactivity.

12.   **Vitamins:** B vitamins and vitamins C, D, and E are essential for children with ADHD. It's important to monitor vitamin levels in your child and to increase his daily intake. The brain relies on vitamin C to produce neurotransmitters like epinephrine and dopamine to increase attention span. Vitamin E improves brain circulation, which is especially beneficial for children with ADHD. Vitamin D is beneficial if moodiness and depression are issues. It also helps with cognitive and psychological problems. Exposing your child to direct sunlight at least 15 minutes per day will increase the level of vitamin D in his system.

13.   **Valerian:** Valerian is yet another herb that has the effect of bringing down hyperactivity to normalcy. Valerian possesses calming properties that the nervous system of a child with ADHD can benefit from.

Chapter 21: The Relationship Between Caffeine & Adhd

Everyone knows that having ADHD can make it very difficult to concentrate. People who suffer from ADHD may have a more difficult time performing certain tasks. They might get distracted easily and become frustrated when performing tasks that take a long time. Living with ADHD can be pretty difficult if medical professionals aren't properly treating you.

ADHD impacts the lives of both children and adults. Many people think of ADHD as something that children have to deal with, but it's actually very prevalent among adults. As many as 4.4% of American adults have ADHD, but many choose not to seek treatment. Knowing this, it should come as no surprise that some people choose to self-medicate instead.

To be clear, the best thing that you can do when you have ADHD is to seek medical treatment. Prescription medications and therapy are the best ways to deal with

ADHD. Other remedies and treatments are not going to be nearly as useful. That being said, a surprising number of people turn to caffeine to try to help with their ADHD symptoms. Most ADHD medications are prescription drugs that act as stimulants. Caffeine is also a type of stimulant, so it should work okay to help people with their ADHD problems, right? Well, you shouldn't get too far ahead of yourself. Caffeine is a very popular way to increase your focus, but it isn't really going to be a great substitute for ADHD treatment. Take a look at the relationship between caffeine & ADHD below to learn more.

What Does Caffeine Do

Using caffeine for ADHD may not be the best choice overall. You need to understand what caffeine is doing to your brain in order to get how it works. Caffeine has the potential to raise your dopamine levels in your brain. Many ADHD medications do this in order to increase the focus on the patient. In theory, caffeine can work as an ADHD medication but it doesn't come without its downsides.

There are many side effects associated with drinking too much caffeine. When you drink a significant amount of caffeinated beverages, you'll run the risk of getting migraine headaches. To add to this, you may also experience insomnia, general irritability, and stomach problems. You'd likely have to drink a lot of caffeine in order to truly replace traditional ADHD medications, making using caffeine as an ADHD drug impractical.

Researchers do think that caffeine may have some potential as an ADHD drug in the future. Tests have been performed on lab rats that show promise. Some of these tests have shown an increased ability to focus in rats that have received caffeine. Having something work well on lab rats is different from having it work for humans who suffer from ADHD, though.

Using coffee for ADHD is probably not going to be the best solution. This doesn't mean that you can't enjoy caffeinated beverages, though. You should speak to your doctor about how caffeine will interact with your ADHD medication. You should be able to enjoy a certain amount of caffeine every day without it being a detriment.

Caffeine and Children

You should definitely avoid letting your kids have too much caffeine. There are some parents who have used caffeine as a substitute for traditional ADHD medicine when treating their children. This doesn't work out well as the side effects of drinking too much caffeine are more pronounced in children. Some evidence shows that caffeine can negatively impact brain development in children too.

Do your best to help your child avoid caffeine if they have ADHD. There might be some signs that high amounts of caffeine will calm hyperactivity, but this is going to come with many side effects. For example, it can make insomnia really bad. Too much caffeine could ruin your child's sleep patterns and they may wind up struggling to stay awake during the day.

Traditional ADHD medication is much better at regulating things. The side effects are not as problematic and you'll be able to keep your child on track. Does caffeine help ADHD? It might in some ways, but it isn't worth the problems that it will cause for your child.

Work together with doctors to come up with the best treatment plan for your kids. This will likely involve traditional stimulant medication. Some kids don't react well to stimulant medications for ADHD, though. There are children who need to be treated with non-stimulant medication, making it even more obvious that caffeine is not likely going to be the best answer.

Caffeine Makes Me Tired ADHD

Some people with ADHD get tired when they drink too much caffeine. This is not usually going to be due to drinking the caffeine itself. The tiredness is going to occur due to losing sleep because of the caffeine that you've taken into your system. If you drink a lot of caffeine throughout your day, then you might have more problems with getting enough sleep.

Not being able to sleep at night can lead to restlessness. You might wind up only getting a few hours of sleep and this will throw off your entire sleeping schedule. Sleep deprivation due to caffeine consumption is more common than you may realize. Caffeinated drinks are very popular and many people consume them at inappropriate times.

To add to this, caffeine has the potential to make those with ADHD more wired than they need to be. You might wind up feeling like you're crashing after being very amped up for a small period of time. It's best to use caffeine sparingly when you have ADHD issues. Try to only drink coffee or soda in the morning and stick to only drinking a reasonable amount.

If you drink caffeine properly, then it might give you a small boost in the morning. You just need to avoid having too much to avoid the negative side effects. As mentioned earlier, consult your family physician on caffeine use and how it might interact with any medications you're taking. It's always best to err on the side of caution.

What About Other Stimulants

Now that you know more about caffeine, you might be curious about whether or not other stimulants will be safe to take. You should always consult your family physician before trying anything new. There are some natural remedies that have proven to be capable of improving focus. Many people buy herbs such as Gingko Biloba in order to help themselves stay on task.

The problem with this is that the natural remedies are still not going to be as effective as the prescription medication. In most cases, you're going to be well-served by following your doctor's plans. If your doctor thinks that a certain medication is worth trying, then you should do your best to trust in them. They have experience and they know how to help people manage their ADHD symptoms.

Chapter 22: Building Mindset

People believe in a growth mindset that their most basic skills can be established through dedication and hard work; the brains and talent are just the starting point. This point of view generates a love of learning and resilience, which is necessary for great achievement.

6.1 What Is Mindfulness?

Will you clear your mind, or focus on one thing? The Mindful Definition of Mindfulness is here. Compassion. It is a very straight word. This means that the mind attends entirely to what is happening, to what you are doing, to the room in which you are going. That may sound trivial, with the exception of the disturbing fact that we so frequently veer from the matter. Our mind is fleeing, we're losing touch with our body, and we're getting stuck in obsessive thoughts about something that's just happening or worrying about the future pretty soon. And that makes us nervous.

Mindfulness is the important human capacity to be fully present, mindful of where we are and what we are doing and not too sensitive or distracted by what is happening around us.

Yet no matter how far we drift go, there is a sense of consciousness right there to snap us back to where we are and what we feel and do. If you want to know what knowledge is, try it for a while at first because terms are hard to nail down.

Definition of Mindfulness:

Mindfulness is the basic capacity of the human being to be fully present, aware of where we are and what we are doing and not overly sensitive or irritated by what is happening around us.

Mindfulness is a quality already possessed by every human being, it's not something you have to conjure up, and you just have to know how to access it.

Although awareness is innate, it can be developed by validated strategies such as sitting, walking, standing and moving meditation (it is also possible to lie down but often leads to sleep); short breaks that we integrate into daily life; and mixing meditation practice with other activities such as yoga or sports.

As we meditate, dwelling on the benefits does not help, just actually doing the practice, and yet there are advantages, or no one would do it. Through studying our own minds, we reduce stress, enhance performance, gain insight and understanding, and increase our sensitivity to the well-being of others.

Meditation of mindfulness offers us a moment in our lives when we can suspend judgment and unleash our natural curiosity about the workings of the mind, presenting our experience to ourselves and others with compassion and kindness.

6.2 How to gain mindfulness and why should you care

8 Things to Learn about mindfulness:

Caution is neither mysterious nor exotic. We are familiar with it because it is what we are already doing, how we are now. This takes a lot of types and goes by many names.

Mindfulness is not something we do particularly added. We already have the opportunity to be there, and it does not demand that we alter who we are. But we can develop these inherent qualities with practical activities that are scientifically proven to benefit us, our loved ones, our friends and neighbors, the people with whom we interact, and we engage in

They don't have to adjust. Solutions that are challenging us to change who we are or become something that we have failed repeatedly. Mindfulness acknowledges and cultivates the best of people we are.

Mindfulness has the ability to become a social phenomenon which is changing.

Anybody can do it. The practice of mindfulness cultivates universal human qualities and requires that none change their beliefs. Everyone can benefit, and the learning is easy.

It is a way of life. Carefulness is more than pure exercise. This brings awareness and empathy to all that we do, and it cuts down unnecessary stress. Even a little does improve our lives.

It's basing on facts. We don't have to take confidence to heart. All research and experience demonstrate their positive health, satisfaction, job, and relationships benefits.

It is sparking creativity. When we deal with the increasing complexity and uncertainty of our environment, being aware will lead us to efficient, resilient, low-cost solutions to seemingly intransigent issues.

How to Be Mindful?

Mindfulness has a complicated way of looking. It's just anything but.

"Mindfulness pays attention in a particular way: consciously, non-judgmentally in the present moment," there are many simple ways in which you can be more conscious. Here are tips for integrating into your everyday life.

1. Practice Mindfulness during Daily Activities:

Try to raise awareness of the day-to-day tasks you typically do on autopilot, for example, pay more attention as you brush your teeth, take a shower, eat breakfast or go to work. From these tasks, zero in on the sight, sound, smell, taste and feel. The daily operation is perhaps more fascinating than you thought.

2. Keep It Short:

Our brains respond better to mindfulness outbursts. So it's more important to be conscious many times a day than a long session or even a weekend retreat. While 20 minutes seem to be the gold standard, it's OK too to start at a few minutes a day.

For example, you can tune into your body, such as concentrating on "how your shoes feel at your feet at that moment, or paying attention to how your jaw is doing [such as, is it] close, loose, or hanging open at the person's audaciousness in the coffee line before you?

3. Practice Patience When Waiting:

Throughout our fast-paced lives, waiting is a huge source of frustration—whether you're waiting in line or traffic-stuck. But while it might sound like a hassle, waiting is, in fact, an opportunity to be conscious. He mentioned turning your attention to your breath when you're waiting. Concentrate on "the rhythm of the air in and out of your body, from moment to moment, and let it be all else, even if there is impatience or frustration."

4. Choose A Prompt to Remind You to Be Conscious of It:

Choose a trigger you regularly encounter to move the brain to mindful mode. For starters, you can pick some doorway or mirror, or use coffee or tea as a reminder.

5. Learn to Meditate:

Formal training in meditation is the best way to develop mindfulness in everyday life. Practicing meditation is how to learn the language of mindfulness. "With little effort, meditation helps us tap into awareness. Even taking 5 minutes to sit still and follow your breath will help you feel more relaxed and connected throughout the rest of your day.

6. Focus On One Thing at A Time:

Studies have found that tasks take 50 per cent longer when multi-tasking with 50 per cent more errors, so consider "uni-tasking" wherever possible, with breaks in between.

7. Slow Down:

Save the cycle, whether it's writing a report, drinking a cup of tea or cleaning up wardrobes. Deliberate and careful attention to day-to-day actions promotes healthy focus and can keep you from feeling overwhelmed.

8. Eat Mindfully:

Having your meal in front of you without the TV, screen or book, where you can really taste and appreciate what you're having, is healthy, not just for your body, but for your soul too.

9.Keep in balance Mobile and Computer Time.

With all media at our disposal, we can quickly be overloading the details. Set screen time limits with defined social networking times (even setting the alarm) and do your best to keep mobile devices out of reach at bedtime.

10. Move:

Whether it's walking, practicing yoga, or just stretching at your desk, you'll be aware of the sensations of your body moving.

11. Spend Time in Nature:

Take walks through parks, woods, mountain trails or beaches, wherever you can be outdoors. It's good for body, mind and spirit to get outside and hold you at the moment.

Mindfulness Basics Practice:

Mindfulness helps us to put some space between ourselves and our reactions, breaking down our conditioned answers. Throughout the day, here's how to tap into your mindfulness:

1. Set some time aside. To access your mindfulness skills, you don't need a meditation pillow or table, or any kind of special equipment but you need to set aside some time and room.

2. Observe the moment, as it is. The purpose of mindfulness is not to quiet the mind or to try to attain an eternal calm state. The objective is simple: we aim to pay attention to the present moment, without any judgment. We know it's easier said than done.

3. Let the decisions roll in. Through our practice, when we find assumptions occur, we should make a mental note of them and let them pass.

4. Go back to observing the moment as it is. Sometimes our minds get carried away

in thought. That's why the goal of mindfulness is to return to the present moment, again and again.

5. Be kind to the wandering conscience. Do not blame yourself for whatever thoughts you have come up with, just practice noticing when your mind has wandered away, and bring it back gently.

This is education. It has been said often that this is very simple, but it is not necessarily secure. The role is just to keep on doing it. Returns are to accrue.

Why It's Important?

Some of the most common mindfulness theories are just plain wrong. You can find the experience very different from what you expected when you start practicing it.

Five things people's mindfulness gets wrong:

1. Paying attention is not about "fixing" you

2. Paying attention is not about avoiding your thoughts

3. Mindfulness is not part of a religion

4. Caution is not an escape from Reality

5. Discretion isn't a panacea

Mindfulness Is About More than Stress Reduction:

Stress Reduction is often an outcome of the practice of mindfulness, but the ultimate goal is not to reduce stress. Awakening to the inner workings of our intellectual, emotional, and physical processes is the aim of mindfulness.

Mindfulness stimulates creativity:

Whether it's writing, drawing or coloring, they all have meditative practices that go with them. We should extend attention to the creative process too.

Mindfulness enhances neural connections:

Through training our brains in mindfulness and related activities, we are able to build new neural pathways and networks within the brain, improving focus, flexibility and awareness. Well-being is an acquired skill.

To reinforce the neural connections, try this simple meditation.

6.3 Be Mindful About ADHD

The study showed that focus training significantly reduced symptoms of ADHD and improved areas of executive function, self-compassion and mental health. Of note, about 16 per cent of the study participants dropped out. A larger trial is needed, but the small study is part of the emerging evidence that carefulness therapies may play a significant role in ADHD treatment.

For several factors, it is essential to consider non-medication treatments parallel and in conjunction with conventional ADHD drug treatment. Approximately 10 to 30 per cent of individuals with ADHD do not entirely respond to stimulant drugs, the traditional first-line treatment for ADHD. In addition, people may experience unpleasant stimulant side effects like dry mouth, jitteriness, increased anxiety, or decreased appetite. While healthy, stimulant medicines often carry the risk of overuse or dependence and cardiovascular risk. Many people may prefer to consider a non-medication approach for managing their ADHD symptoms for these reasons.

A recent review found a substantial clear benefit in young adults from CBT mindfulness as an adjunct therapy paired with traditional ADHD drug treatment. Of the 12 trials released over the past five years, most results showed a decrease in frequency for ADHD with the introduction of CBT mindfulness to standard treatment.

While research is needed in this field, these recent studies suggest a promising and evolving role of mindfulness in the treatment of ADHD.

6.4 Control Mindfulness and Focus On Self-Regulation

It is possible to define self-regulation in different ways. This means regulating one's actions, feelings, and thoughts in the pursuit of long term goals in the most basic sense. Emotional self-regulation more precisely refers to the ability to control destructive feelings and impulses. In other words, think before you act. It also represents the desire to cheer up after deceptions and work in a manner compatible with your deepest held beliefs.

Self-regulatory development:

Your capacity to self-regulate as an adult has its roots in your childhood development. Understanding how to self-regulate is an essential skill that kids learn for both emotional maturity and later on social connections.

In an ideal situation, an infant who throws tantrums grows into a child who knows how to handle uncomfortable feelings without throwing a fit and later on into an adult who can control urges to behave on the basis of unpleasant feelings. Maturity ultimately represents the capacity with maturity and thoughtfulness to face mental, social, and cognitive challenges in the world. If this definition reminds you of awareness, it's not unintentional awareness that is actually related to self-regulating capacity.

Importance:

Self-regulation requires pausing between feelings, and taking the time to think things over, making a strategy, patiently wait. Kids may struggle with these behaviors, and adults too.

It's easy to see how failure to self-regulate will cause liver problems. A child who out of rage screams or hits other children will not be familiar with peers, and may face reprimands in school. A person with poor self-regulation skills may lack self-confidence and self-esteem and may experience stress and frustration while dealing with issues. This may often be expressed in terms of anger or anxiety and could be diagnosed as a mental disorder in more severe cases.

Self-regulation is also critical in that it helps you to behave and express yourself adequately in accordance with your deeply held beliefs or social conscience. If you value academic achievement, it will encourage you to plan, rather than slack off, before a test. When you appreciate helping others, even if you are on a tight deadline yourself, it will encourage you to maintain a coworker with a project.

Self-regulation, in its most basic form, allows us to bounce back from defeat, and to remain calm under pressure. Those two talents, more than any other abilities, can take you through life.

Common Problems:

How are self-regulatory problems developing? It could start early; being ignored as a child. A child who does not feel comfortable and secure, or who is uncertain if his or her needs will be met, may have difficulty relieving and self-regulating. Later, an infant, teen or adult may struggle with self-regulation, either because that skill was not established during childhood, or because of a lack of strategies to handle painful feelings. When left unchecked, this could contribute over time to more serious problems such as mental health disorders and risky behaviors such as substance abuse.

How to Put Self-Regulation in Practice:

You probably think that being good at self-regulating sounds wonderful, but you still don't know how to improve your skills.

Parents can help in children develop self-regulation through rituals (e.g. setting sure mealtimes, providing a set of behaviors for each activity). Routines help kids learn what to expect so they can feel comfortable. If children act in ways that do not show self-regulation, ignore their wishes, such as, if they disrupt a conversation, making them wait.

The first step to self-regulation as an adult is to understand that everyone has a choice on how to respond to circumstances. While you may feel like life has handed you a bad hand, what matters most is not the hand you are given, but how you react to it. How exactly do you learn that self-regulation skill?

Recognize that you have three choices in every situation: approach, avoidance and attack. While it may seem like your behavioral choice is beyond your control, it is not. You may be more swayed by your feelings towards one direction, but you are more than just those feelings.

The second step is to become conscious of your fleeting feelings. Would you wish to run away from a difficult situation? Would you feel like killing someone who hurt you in anger? Track the body to get answers as to how you behave when it's not immediately apparent to you. For example, a heart that proliferates may be an indication that you are entering a state of rage or a panic attack.

Begin restoring equilibrium by concentrating on your deeply held beliefs, rather than those feelings that are transitory. Look beyond that discomfort to the bigger picture at the moment. Then, act in a manner corresponding to self-regulation.

A Word from Very well:

Once you've mastered this delicate balancing act, you're going to start self-regulating more often, and it's going to become a way of life for you. Developing self-regulation skills will strengthen your strength and ability to face tough life circumstances. Nonetheless, consider visiting a mental health professional if you feel that you cannot teach yourself how to self-regulate. The time to incorporate specific strategies for your situation may be helpful.

Chapter 24: Can Children With Adhd Get Better?

Children with ADHD can get better with treatment, but there is no cure. There are three basic types of treatment:

Medication. Several medications can help. The most common types are called stimulants. Medications help children focus, learn, and stay calm. Some parents do not want to use medications because they do not like the side effects others think the older children will get hooked on it.

Sometimes medications cause side effects, such as sleep problems or stomachaches. Your child may need to try a few medications to see which one works best. It's important that you and your doctor watch your child closely while he or she is taking medicine.

Therapy. There are different kinds of therapy. Behavioral therapy can help teach children to control their behavior so they can do better at school and at home.

Medication and therapy combined**.**

Some parents may prefer to combine medication and therapy at the same time.

Teenagers and ADHD

Most teens with ADHD are embarrassed with the diagnosis of having ADHD.

Many of them deny that they have ADHD because they may feel different from their friends. Teens are also facing other challenges at this time discovering their identity, dealing with peer pressure and other things that are going on in their lives.

They also need to focus on organization skills and academic issues. The teen should be told that having ADHD is not their fault nor is it caused by something they may have done.

Teens may also have poor self-esteem, feel stressed, tired and feel their parents did not understand them. They may also tell you there is nothing wrong with me. I am fine they may even refuse to take their medications.

Teen age years are very challenging for most parents, but the teenager with ADHD this is an even more trying time for them. They are now faced with trying to find their identity, schooling, trying to fit in with others, making and keeping new friends so for these children this is much harder for them to handle.

These children now desire to be independent and try doing things like using drugs, becoming sexually active and using alcohol which can lead to bad consequences. Don't forget at this time lots of teenagers are getting their drivers license and using their family vehicles. They pick up friends drink alcohol and speed the streets causing accidents.

Even though the teenager may be more capable in some ways, in other ways they need to have different rules and adhere to them. Both parents may not agree on what privileges the child may have and start fighting with each other so problems start occurring in the home.

The child should be given rules to adhere to and have consequences if the rules are broken. The rules should also be explained and the reason for the rule. Communication between parent and child is even more important now.

Rules should be posted on the refrigerator or in a convenient location so that the child knows it is there. These teenagers should be able to help with appropriate household chores and other things around the house also.

At this time the teenager will want to spend more time away from home with friends and just doing other things. They will want to demand later curfew and even the use of your vehicle. Listen to what your child is saying, you may also need to negotiate some of the request to come to a better understanding of helping your child to understand what you are relating.

They will resent certain restrictions but you have to be firm if you think it is in your child's best interest. Let them know the rules are to be carried out no matter what or there will be consequences.

These children sometimes become difficult and may not want to take their medications that are prescribed for them or they may not want to eat healthy cooked foods at home. They will want to consume a lot of fast foods to fill their stomachs which is not healthy for them.

Guide your child and try to understand what they are going through. Help them to make good choices. Avoid punishing your child every time he/she does something wrong or break the rules. Let your child know you are always there for them and they can come to you even if it is just to talk.

Even though the symptoms of ADHD may change as the child grows, teens with ADD/ADHD still require treatment and may need treatment into adulthood.

Depression and **the** ADHD Child

Depression is defined as an illness when the feelings of sadness, hopelessness, and despair persist and interfere with a child or adolescent's ability to function normally.

Some depression is normal in people lasts for a short period of time such as when a family member dies, or there is a divorce in the family. You freeze and don't know what to think or what to feel so you become numb and depressed. But this phase eventually passes as time goes by.

About 5% of adolescence and teenagers suffer from depression but the risk of a child with ADHD, learning and conduct disorders are much greater. Depression and ADHD can be treated with medications and behavior therapies.

Over time depression has become more common and is now recognized in younger children. Suicide rate in the teens increases as the depression rate increases. Mental health professionals advise parents to be aware of signs of depression in their children.

Some signs of depression in the teenager may be frequent sadness, crying or tearful spells, they may want to be alone most times and don't talk much. Teens may be writing poetry with morbid themes.

Self-Injury

Teens that have difficulty talking about their feelings may show their emotional tension, physical discomfort, pain and low self-esteem by cutting themselves.

They may feel hopeless like life is not worth living, do not take pride in their appearance and hygiene. They may also believe that a negative behavior will not change and so does not care about the future.

Children may drop out from activities they once enjoyed sometimes they even drop out of school.

They may live an isolated life and not willing to spend time with friends and families. Most of these children do not share their feelings as they feel no one is really listening to them and would not understand them.

There may be low energy and boredom in classes and so they miss classes and fail in school. These children often cause trouble at home or at school and not know they are depressed.

Parents do not think about their children being depressed and so a diagnosis of depression goes unnoticed. Parents are so busy trying to put a roof over their family and feed them that they hardly notice what is going on with their child.

These children are often depressed, angry or hostile with most of their anger projected towards their parents.

Sometimes teens may run away from home not because they want to run away but because they want help and do not know how to ask for it.

Because the child may not always seem sad, parents and teachers may not realize that the behavior problem is a sign of depression.

The teenager may talk about suicide or say things like they should be dead, or I want to kill myself, if you hear a child saying these things always take it seriously and seek help.

Some children may turn to drugs, alcohol and promiscuity, as a way out.

Chapter 25: The Dangers Of Using Cbd Oil In An Individual With Adhd

In a majority of cases of individuals using CBD oil, there have been no major negative side effects. This is not to say it is entirely without side effects.

Each person experiences their own individual set of ADHD symptoms. The reason for consulting with doctors about the illness is that not all individuals respond to medications or treatments the same way.

Two people with ADHD might experience different reactions to the same medical prescription, one finding relief, the other not.

The same can be said of CBD oil. How an individual reacts is sometimes their own unique experience and there is no guarantee that two people will experience the same relief.

Some people who have taken CBD oil, regardless of whether it was for ADHD or not, experience some of the following symptoms:

Nausea or changes in their appetite (some experienced an increase while others experienced a decrease)

Irritability or swift changes in mood

Fatigue or drowsiness

Diarrhea

Dry mouth

Some of these effects might coincide with the symptoms of ADHD, to a negative effect.

Another challenge with CBD oil is in relation to the manufacture of the product. While federal law stipulates that CBD must contain less than .3% THC, it is difficult to regulate the vast amount of CBD products hitting the market.

There is not one specific uniform dosage or ratio that exists among the federal regulations. So, while manufacturers may indeed stick with the .3% THC requirement, products might not actually contain as much CBD as the buyer thinks.

The regulations lack specificity on how many milligrams of CBD a single dropper should contain. In one study, it was revealed that around 26% of CBD products on the market contain less CBD than advertised.

This makes it dosing and finding the effective amount of CBD to take challenging. If directions say half a dropper, or.5mg, that's not to say every bottle contains the same strength of CBD and delivers the same dose.

A high concentration of CBD oil might be mixed with a small amount of coconut oil, for example, with a specific set of directions, while a lower concentrated product might have a higher amount of coconut oil and less CBD and no instructions. There is a clear level of inconsistencies on the market.

This is not to say that CBD oil is dangerous in any way. Studies and personal testamonials have shown there to be very little in the way of side effects or dangers. What's important is that a buyer know the source, research the source, and question the source, to be able to gather as much information for themselves as possible.

Conclusions

With all the strategies offered in the previous chapters, many of them can be adapted to your particular situation. There are also a few strategies that are applicable to any situation involving a person with ADHD.

Strategy 13: Have A Plan B

The truth is that life happens and sometimes in the not-so-expected way. You can lay the best plans, have the best treatment protocol in place and – BOOM – life happens. Stability and consistency are crucial to the management of ADHD symptoms. Having a Plan B will give you peace of mind that if A isn't an option, B is in the wings and ready to go. One less thing to worry about.

Strategy 14: Ask For Help

Having ADHD or a loved one who does can be intensely emotional and stressful. It can turn your world upside down and leave you feeling alone. Therapy is not just for someone with a diagnosis. Therapy can also offer help to those who love a person with ADHD. Sometimes having a neutral person that will listen to those deep, personal through we'd never say out loud is healing and empowering. There is no shame in seeking help if you need it.

Strategy #15: You Are Not Your Diagnosis

ADHD only defines you (or your loved one) if allowed to do so. Remember that ADHD is a label of sorts used to describe a disorder and set of symptoms. It is not the person. Labels describe. They do not define. A person is so much more complex and all of the things you love about you are inside. You have a name. You have a story. You have a life to live. Acknowledge your symptoms, get a treatment plan in place and let the people who love you love you ADHD and all.